東洋文庫 監修

重要文化財

ジョン・セーリス『日本渡航記』

Saris, John
The first voyage of theEnglish to the Islands of Japan, 1617.

東洋文庫善本叢書
第二期　欧文貴重書③

勉誠出版

目　次

ジョン・セーリス『日本渡航記』　影印 …………………………………………………… 3

ジョン・セーリス『日本渡航記』　解説 ……………………………… 平野健一郎　147

凡　例

・公益財団法人東洋文庫所蔵の「ジョン・セーリス『日本渡航記』」を原色・原寸で影印した。
・解説は、平野健一郎（東洋文庫）が担当した。
・本書掲載のすべての画像は東洋文庫および勉誠出版の許可なく二次使用することを禁じる。

VOYAGE TO JAPAN

背

小口

天

地

The first voiage of

the English to the Islands of JAPAN.

Being the eighth voyage

to the East Indies, vnder the Commaund of Captaine
John Saris of London, with three Shipps, The Cloue,
the Hector, and the Thomas, Manned with 262
men. Begun, Aprill 18. 1611. And
finished September 27. 1614.

※ ※

Wherein are particulerly related

diuers matters worthy of obseruation, both for
Course, and Action during the said voiage.

※ ※

With what befell them in the Red Sea, Bantam,
in Iaua Maior, the Moluccæ Islands, the Islande
of Japan, by th'inhabitants called Neffon, the
manner of theire entertainement there, and discovery
of the Country 800 miles within land, the setling of
an English Factorie, at Firando, with their
returne home alonge the Coast
of CHINA.

;;;

Togeather with the Coppies of the Greate Turkes Passe,
and Patent for Priuiledges obtayned of the Emperor
of the Islands of Japan for our English nation,
trading thither, and of the Kings Maiesties letters &
Presents, as alsoe of the like from the Emperour of
JAPAN, and from the Kinge of FIRANDO,
to his Highnes. 1617.

※ ※

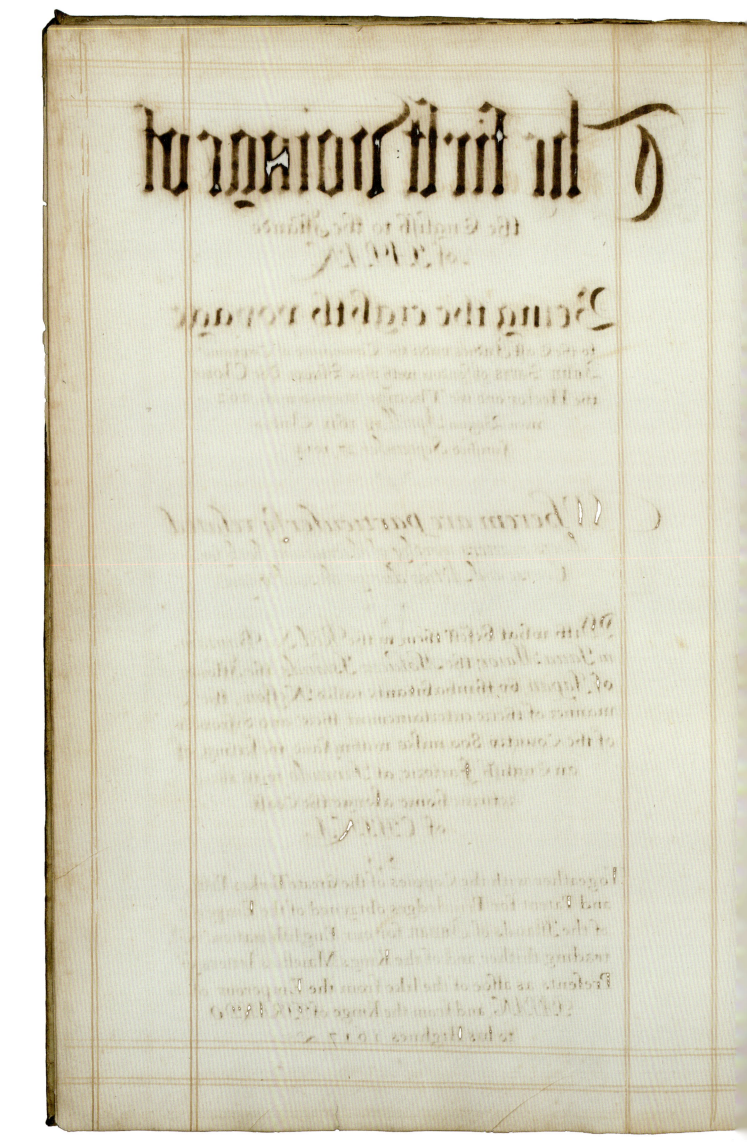

To the right honorable Sir
ffrauncis Bacon knight, Lord Keeper of the greate Seale of England, and one of his ma:ts most honorable Privy Councell.

Right honorable.

Such is the valewe of yo:r Lordshipps pretious time, as might make it too much presumption in me to vsurpe the least parte thereof, were it not in his dispensation who knowing best howe to vse it, knowes also best howe to proportion it. May it then please your honor from your higher Orbe, to cast an eye vpon the wandring course of a lower Planet, where your Lp: may viewe in a fewe howers, what was discovered in diuers yeares. It hath hitherto lien in obscuritie, though vnder the Survey of M:r Richard Hackluit, a man industrious and well deseruing of such whose mindes are not whollie confined at home, his too indulgent approbation had pressed it for publique vse, but death prevented him. his last charge (which to neglect were irreligious) made it surviue, and me soe hardie as to present it to your Lps viewe; not presuming vpon the worth of it, but your honors generous disposition, to whome it can appeare in noe posture of art or industrie that can be exempt from a ray of y:t goodnes wherein yo:r Lp: farre exceedes your well deserved greatnes, to which if I may add the truth which confirmed by future relations shall vindicate it selfe from the common imputation, I hope it shall excuse what hath escaped amisse from him whoe could finde no better meanes at the present to expresse his forwardnes to doe yo:r Hono:r seruice, and should thinck himself happie after long travell to rest vnder soe auspitious an influence. The Almightie continewe to your Lordshipp increase of blessinges and hono:r till it be consumate in Glory

Yo:r hono:r: devoted in his best of seruice

J: Saris.

		From England to Madagascar.
1611.		
Aprill.	18	

The Eighteenth day of

Aprill Anno 1611. wee sett saile out of the Downes.

June	6.	The 6th of June following wee passed the Equinoctiall Lyne.
August	1.	The first of August 1611. wee arived in the Bay of Saldania where having well refreshed our selves the space of 8 daies.
August	9.	The 9th of August in the morning wee waighed Anker, and about fower in the afternoone, were five leagues of the Cape Buena Esperansa.
	10.	Latitude 35 degrees 31 minutes, way Sotherly, 38 leagues, winde at W.N.W. heere wee felt a current setting to the westward.
	11.	Variation at sunne setting, 5 degrees 29 minutes westerlie.
	12.	is 36 degrees 03 minutes Lattitude
	16.	Latt: 37d 19 minutes, way Sotherly, winde N.E. & N.N.E. & verie extreame foule weather with thunder and lightening. The like weather to the 20th with rayne extreamelie.
	23.	wee shipt such an extreame sea as that it did splitt the greatest parte of our mayne course out of the Bolt ropes. The shipps way N.E. ¼ esterlie, the winde at N.W. and at S.S.W. a greatt storme.
	24.	Lat: 31d 36 minutes way N.E. winde at N.N.W. variation at sunne rising 8d 44 minutes westerly.
	26.	Lat: 29d 45 minutes way N.E. 17 leagues Variation 13. 20. m. westerlie, winde at S.E.
	27.	Lat: 29d 33 minutes Course N.E. ¼ Easterlie. 15 leagues, the winde N. and N. by W. faier weather.
	29.	Lat: 29d 56 minutes, way N.E. by E. 9 leagues. Winde S.E. and at night S.W. Variation at Sunne rising 15d 17 minutes westerlie.
September	2.	Lat: 24d 21 minutes way E by N. northerlie, 6 leagues Nota. That since our comming from Cape B. Speranza wee found noe Monsons of West windes (as hath bene reported) but to the contrarie did finde, rayne Thunder and lightening; yet at that present verie faier and soe hott that Calmes were to be doubted. And the wind N. Ely S. Ely. and Ely.

.1611.   Madagascar.

| September | 3 | Lat. 23^d. 50^m. way S. by W. 23 leagues, winde at S. About 5. at night wee made land, being the Island of Madagascar, otherwise called St. Laurence, the Bay of St. Augustine, bearing E. by N: about 6 leagues off. And then stood away N. N: E: Variation at sunne setting 15^d. 11^m westerlie. Wee sounded but had noe ground at 100. fathum, the land not very high but sandy. And then wee passed the Tropique of Capricorne, to the N ward. |

The Bay of St Augustine in ye Isle of St Laurence

7. Lat. 19^d. 35^m. way N. N: W: 48 leagues, the winde at S. wee steered N. by W.

8. Lat. 17^d. 58^m. way N. by W. 36. L. winde S. Variation 14^d 20^m westerlie. Nota, heere wee supposed to be in a Current setting to ye N ward. For these last 24 howers wee deprest the S. Pole 2^d. 37^m. which otherwise had ben impossible, it having byn for the most parte Calme.

9. Lat. 17^d. 29^m. way N by W. ¼ westerly 10 L. the winde at S. The Sunnes Amplitude observed, made the Var: 13^d. 53^m. westerly.

10. Lat. 17^d. 03^m. way N W 12 L. winde at N. E. wee steered N. N. W. Var: at sunne rising 13^d. 54 ^{m} westerly. Nota, heere wee found a strong Current setting S. S. W. for these last 24 howers shee could not haue runn lesse then 24 leagues, having a stiff gale, but for the reason aforesaid. In the evening wee made the Island Primeiras, bearing W by N about 4 leagues off.

A strong Current

11. Lat. 17^d. 33^m. way S. by E. ½ a point Easterly 14 L: the winde at N. E. and N. E. by E. a storme.

Nota. that having stood but one watch and a halfe to the E: warde, the current did carrie vs 30 ^{m}. to the S. warde, of the Lat: wee were in by the last observation. Then wee stoode in for the land N. N. W. hoping of a better winde neere the shoare with lesse current, and suddenly the water changed but wee could finde noe ground at 100 fathom. In the evening wee made the land, bearing N and N by W. about 6. leagues off: finding it to be the Islandes Primeiras, but being to the N ward of it, it shewed somewhat longer then before, for it did beare from the N. W. to the N of vs. Wee sounded and had 20. fathum small glistering sand, and sounding had 20 fathum black oaze with black shells. Then wee stood of to the E ward the storme continuing wth more winde in the night then in the daie. And having stoode of one glasse wee sounded and had 22 fathum gray sand and shells.

Islands Primeiras

12. Lat. 18. 17 ^{m}. way S. E by E. 28 L. winde at N. E. a storme, soe that these last 24 howers wee were carried by force of the current 44 ^{m}. to the S. ward of the former observation. Var. 14^d. 41. ^{m}. westerly. About night the winde veared to the E. N. E. soe that wee lay N. wth
the

1611   **The Ilands de Angoxa**

the stemm.

September 13. Lat: 19°. 16ᵐ way, S: E: by S: 22 leagues, winde N. E: by E: little winde, the current very strong against vs.

15. Lat: 16°. 46ᵐ way N. N. E: ½ point easterly, 30 leagues, winde S: W: wee steered N. E: by N. *Nota.* Heere wee found the current soe terrible, for wee haue deprest the pole 1°. 27 minutes in these 24 howers. The reason wee supposed to be that the Island Iuan de nova was betweene vs and the current, for wee made accompt it did beare E: by N: 18 leagues off. *Var:* at sunne setting 12°. 08ᵐ westerly.

16. Lat: 16°. 09ᵐ way N. N. E: 18 leagues wee steered N. E: by N. winde S: W: by S: little winde, but a stronge current, *Var:* at Sunne setting 13°. 03ᵐ westerlie.

The Islands de Angoxa —

17. The shipps waie N by W. 8 leagues. *Var:* 12°. 01ᵐ westerly. in the morne wee made the land to the S ward of Mosambique making it to be the Islandes de Angoxa bearing W: S: W: 7 leagues. The westermost parte of the said Islandes seeming whitish. The mayne to the Northward, bearing N. by E: smooth champion ground, wee steered N. E. by E. and towardes eueninge wee sawe the land trenting to the N ward, seeming to the seaward to be full of trees. Heere wee founde the current to sett N. N. W. for wee could perceaue by the land that wee rann very fast to the N: ward, and hauing little winde wee sounded often, but could finde no grounde at 100 fathum.

18. Lat: 15°. 14ᵐ way N. E: by E. 7 leagues, wee steered N. E. the winde at S. W. the reason wee deprest the pole 26ᵐ was, that wee were neere the shoare, with the head land of Mosambique, from whence the current setts.

An extreame current to the Southwarde —

19. Lat: 15°. 29ᵐ way S: by E. 4 leagues winde at E. S. E. wee steered N. E. but by extremitie of the current wee were turned to the S ward: soe that wee were heere 10 daies and could not gett to the Northward notwithstanding wee had a faier and reasonable stiff gale.

A very dange= rous shoale.

21. Lat: 16. 20ᵐ waie S: by W. 4 leagues winde N. E: and N. E: by E: little winde. In the morne wee were neerer the Northernemost of the Islandes de Angoxas, bearing W: by W. N. about 3 leagues of. And to windeward of vs wee espied a verie dangerous shoale, lying E. of the N. parte of the mayne at the least 3 pointes into the sea having a drit splatt of white sand betweene it and the maine. Wee sounded and had grounde at 30 fathum: redd stones like turrall with graie sand, and shells, wee stud of it being a lee shoare, and a westerlie current.

Heere the Maryne Counsell was assembled to whome was propounded that hauing byn 10 daies vppon the coast of Mosambique, and by violence of the S. S. W. current and E: windes misseted much to the Southward of our former Lat: and at present neere the shoare, seeing noe daunger but what was open to the viewe, the winde at N. E. that if wee should stand of, wee were likelie to be putt to Leeward, and allmost out of hope of recouering our voiage in any seasonable time and hauing a darke moone then in hand, which caused vs to bee the more fearefull of the shoare, yf wee should not when wee had faier weather, better experience

1611
September.

The Islands de Angoxa

expedient by acquainting our selues therewith. Therefore the readiest way to gayne vs this expperience was held and soe generallie concluded, to stand in and see if there were anie convenient place to Anker in some parte of this Bay, to send our boates abroade to prevent the worst vntill weather and winde would giue vs leaue to plie it vpp, and finding neither the winde to favoure vs, nor place to ride in, Then to stand over for Sanct Lawrence, and there to plie to the N waerde as winde and weather would permitt.

About 4 of the clock in the Eveninge wee were about 4 miles of the Nermost Islands, being lowe sandie grounde full of trees wee sounded, had 30. 24. 18. and 16. fathum, graie sand and redd stones like currull. They are manye Islandes stretching from the W. N. W. to the S. W. by S. or S. S. W. And finding by our Skiffe which was sent of, that the current did sett exceeding stronglie to the S. W. by W. and suth vnexten shoaling, wee stood of for Sanct Laurence.

Nota that these Islandes de Angoxas doe stand 00° 40ᵐ more northerly in the platt, then wee finde them to be by exact observation for in the platt they ly in 15° 40ᵐ and wee finde them in 16° 20ᵐ to the Southward of the Equinoctiall line: Var: 13° 00ᵐ westerlie.

The Islands de Angoxa in 16. d. 20. minuts

22. Lat. 17 degrees 05 minutes way S S. E 18 leagues winde N. E. and in 24 howers that wee parted from the land lost ——— 45ᵐ. But towardes eveninge the winde came to the S. E. and S. E. by S. wee steered N. E. and N. E. by E. and E. N. E. for the Island S. Lawrence looking out for Juan de Noua which Hugh van Linschoten willeth to beware of, and not to come neere it in a smale moone. Notwithstanding wee were inforced to put our selues in hazard, to gett ^but of this Current and dangerous place: Variation at Sunne settinge 12. degrees 44ᵐ westerlie.

23. The 23 Lat. 16°. 24 minutes way N. E. 22 leagues winde at S. S. W. wee steered E. N. E. to ridd vs of the current having deprest the Pole these last 24 howers, 00° 41ᵐ Var: at Sunne settinge 13° 16ᵐ westerly.

24. Lat. 16 degrees 16ᵐ waie E. N. E. 10 leagues winde at S. W. and S. S. E: till 8 in the morning it came then to the N and N. by E. little winde.

25. In the morning at breake of daie (to our greate admiration) wee sawe land to the Westward bearing N. by W. 5 leagues of, not once looking for any that waie, But to the E ward, for Juan de noua which wee made attempt could not be, about 6 leagues south from vs, and being be calmed did doubt least the current would sett vs vpon it in the night but the daie cleeringe wee found it to be the Nothermost Island of the Angoxas, whence wee departed the 21 ditto in the afternoone, which soe amazed our Mariners as that they were discouraged of getting our voiage this waie. The reason of this difference was as wee supposed by a countercurrent which certenlie in the swale of the moone doth sett. E. N. E. and west S. W. from the Plashella or pointe of the shoare which lieth N. E. by E: of the Nothermost parte of Juan de Noua which meeting with our auncient enimy the N. N. E. Current hath thus violentlie put vs ouer to the W wardes notwithstanding wee haue had a fresh gale and faier winde vntill this morning that it fell calme. Nota. that if there be anie such Island as Juan de Noua, it lies not soe farr to the westward as Daniells platts make mention, but standes neerer the mayne Island, otherwise wee must of necessitie haue

seene it

1611   The Islands Primeiras.

September.

25. seene it, They of the 4 voiage in the Assension, made attempt that they passed to the E warde of it, and S.t Laurence, which thing the Portugalls hould impossible saying that it standeth soe neere the mayne Island, as that there is not passage but a little channell which one of their shipps was inforced to put through. And since nor before, they haue not heard of anie to haue donne the like. Wherefore it was held amongest vs to be but a runing of the Portugalls, to plant such an Island soe farr to the westward, to th'end that such as shall saile this waie (being not soe well experienced as themselues) might (giving it a birth,) fall into this extreame current which wee certenlie founde to sett more westerly then N.E. and S.W. Wherefore it is necessarie for all such as shalbe bonnde this waie, to be vppon the Coast of S.t Laurence by the first of June. And from the Cape S.t Augustine vntill they come into 12.d 00.m. to keepe vpp to the E warde and not to make their waie to the W. of the N. or N. by W. for feare of the S.W. current w.th with calmes and 14.d 2.m. Variation westerlie, will per force sett them ouer vppon the coast of Soffala. And most certen it is that in August and September you shall finde verie violent N.E. windes, soe that if you would stand it ouer for S.t Laurence yee shall not fetch it without greate danger of the shoales of Judea (the current taking them on the broadeside) I meane if they be to the N. of the said shoales, neither can yee stopp vppon the ∞ or mayne to keepe your Latitude, for it is broken grounde, and verye deepe water.

A falshood of the Portugales.

Latitude 16 degrees 20 minutes waie N.E. ¼ Easterly 28 leagues, the winde variable, Var: at sunne setting 14.d 24.m. westerly.

26. Latitude 17.d 15 minutes waie 18 leagues, winde at E. and N.E. wee steered S.E. by S. Variation at sunne settinge 13.d 11.m westerlie.

27. Latitude 17.d 10 minutes waie N.N.E. 14 leagues winde E. and E.S.E. in the afternoone wee sawe land bearing N. westerly about 5 mile off, finding it to be the Island Primeiras, which wee departed from y.e 11.th The northermost Island bearing N by E. and the southmost west seemed to be verie smooth grounde and betweene them and the mayne broken ∞ grounde full of freth and steepe. Wee finding no place to Ankor in, hauing Night in hand, stode of the winde at E. and E by N. little winde and stronge current westerlie. Variation 11.d 23 minutes W.

28. Latitude 17.d 26.m way 17 leagues S. by W. winde E.N.E. N.E. by E. and N.E. much winde and a greate sea.

29. Latitude 19.d 22.m way S. 27 leagues winde variable at E.S.E. E. and E by N. a stronge current westerlie and verie much winde. Var: 14.d 02.m westerlie.

30. Latitude 18 degrees. 44 minutes. Way. N.E. 19 leagues winde S.E. wee steered for the most parte. E by N. with a stiff gale, vntill 8. at night, and then S. and S by E. hoping to gett over for S.t Laurence out of the current.

October 1.

October 1611 — The Islands Comora

1. The first, the shipps waie N: E: by E: 20 leagues winde S: and S.S.E: wee steered E: by N: much winde, about noone calme, with much rayne Var: at sunne setting 14.d 17.m westerlie.

2. Lat: 17.d 16.m waie E: N: E: ¼ Northerlie 22 leagues wee steered E: by N: winde S.S.E: and S.E: variation at sunne rising 12.d 39.m westerly, about noone wee made land, bearing N: N: W: about 7 leagues of, & making attempt wee had been over vppon St Laurence in regarde of the course wee kept. But rising in two partes like Islandes wee doubted it was the Island Primeiras and therefore held it fitting to stand to the E: ward albeit it should prove the Islandes Premeiras or Juan de Noua, And soe steered E: by N: and E: N: E: till midnight the winde S: E: and S: E: by E: and in the morninge the winde came to the E: N: E: and N: E: by E: Soe that wee coulde lye but S: E: by E: little winde, keeping our leade everie glasse, but had noe grounde at 100 ffathom.

3. Wee came to an ancker betweene Soffala and Mosambique in 13 and 14 fathum. Lat: 16.d 32.m Longitude 76.d 10.m. Variation 11.d 50.m westerly wee ancked under an Island neere unto the mayne vppon which wee neither founde people nor fresh water, though wee digged verie deept in the sand.

10. wee waied, the winde at S.S.W: and stood over E: by N: for St Laurence hoping thereby to gett out of these currents

Thus were wee tossed to and fro with variable windes and still troubled with the current comming out of the N: E: vntill

The Island Moyella.

26. wee came to an ancker vnder Moyella which is one of the Islands Comora Lat: 12.d 13 minutes to the S: ward of the Equinoctiall where wee refreshed our selues 8 daies procuring Bullocks Goates Hennes Lemmons Cokers, Limes, Papanes, Plantens, Pomgarnetts, sugercanes, Tammarin Hennes, Rice milke, rootes, egges and fish in exchange of smale haberdashery wares and some money, and had heere kinde vsage and greate store of fresh water, the rather, for that wee stood still vppon our guarde.

I invited the king of Moyella being a Mahometane aboord the Clove, and entertained him with a noise of trumpetts and a consorte of musique with a banckett which hee refused to eate of because it was then his Lent, which amongest them is called Rammadam. but hee tooke awaie with him the best of the banckett to carrie to the Queene his mother, sayinge they would eate it, when the sunne was downe.

The Queenes name was Sultanna Mannangassa, The kinges name was Sariffa Babucarree.

Hee requested mee to leave him a lre in his commendacions to those that should happen heereafter to come thether whereby they might vnderstand of his honest dealing with vs The like letter hee had procured from Stephen Verhaghen Admirall of 12 Holland shipps whoe arriued here there in
Anno

1611		The mayne of Melinda
October	26	Anno 1604. which hee deliuered vnto mee and I gaue him the like, with this caution, in the end thereof, that they should not giue too greate credditt to them, but stand vppon theire guard, for that oftentimes weapons confirme peace.
		The inhabitants heere are Negros with short curled haier, with Pintados about theire middells, some wearing white cappes, other Turbants, by which wee knewe them to be Mahometanes.
		The kinge himselfe was apparelled in a white cotten coate, a Turbant vppon his heade and a Guzerat Pintado about his middell hee was little whiter then the ordinarie people whoe are black, Hee was leane, hee had a rounde thynn black bearde, greate eies, of a lowe stature, and of verie fewe wordes, hee could speake a little Arabique, which hee had learned in his Pilgrimage to Meca, from whence hee had the name of Sheriff. Hee desired to continue a vnitie of ffrendshipp with me, and that wee might call Brethren, promising that what his Island affoorded, I should not want.
		Heere they desier money, whereby I vnderstand Spanish Royalls of eight, rather then comoditie. But for Crimson broade cloth, redd stuld cappes, & Cambaya clothes and sword Blades wee maie haue anie thing the Island affoorded which serveth onelie for refreshing, and not maie for marchaundizing and ladinge of shipps.
November	4	Wee sett saile from this Island Moyetta.
	17	In the morning wee made the land being the mayne of Melinde, the Baye or Gulf called Formosa bearing N.W: about 4 leagues of. The land trentinge N:E: and S:W: wee had 30 fathum smale graie sand and shells, Winde at E:N:E: wee stoode of S:E: a stiff gale, and a verie greate sea, which sheweth to the wa be shoale water and a turrent which wee founde to sett alongst the shoare N:E. Latitude 2 degrees 10. minutes. Variation at sunne settinge 12.d: 31. m westerlie.
		Nota: this land lieth more Easterlie then in our platts, otherwise wee should not haue fallen therewith soe soone, for by our reckoninge wee weare at the least 48. leagues of.
	29	Lat: 4d. 44 minutes Var: 17: 34 minutes westerlie, being as wee supposed 12 leagues of, the shoales called Baxos de Malhina. E: by S: wee had a greate ripling, and ouerfall of water as if it had bene shoale water, but soundinge, found not grownde at 100 fathum. The winde came about heere to S:S:E: our course N:E:
December	1	Lat: 03. 40.m way N.N.E: 8. leagues winde at N.N.E: E.S.E: and N.E: by N: little winde, for the most parte calme, and had a verie fearefull rippling of the water, much like vnto the fall at London bridge being out of sight of land and finding not grownd at 100 fathum, when wee stood into the land it left vs, but bearing of (being 50. leagues from land) wee found verie terrible. Variation 16.d: 15 minutes westerlie.

A fearefull rippling of the water.

December. 2.

1611   Melinda to Magadoxa

December

2. Latitude 2d 55m way N.E. by N. 18 leagues winde variable, the riplinge contynuinge. Var. 15d 57 minutes westerlie, which moved us to thinck that wee had a current setting to the west, the Variation decreasinge soe suddenlie.

3. Lat. 4d 4m waie S. 23 leagues winde variable most parte calme with greatt riplinge of the water and a verie stronge current Southerly soe that these last 24 howers wee are carried back to the S.wardes off our former Lat. 01d. 9 minutes.

4. Lat. 4d 33m waie S. 10 leagues little winde and variable betwixt the N.E. and E. by S., verie strange riplinge of the water and stronge current southerlie. Var: 18 degrees 44 minutes westerlie.

5. Lat: 4d 54m way S by E. 7 leagues winde variable betwixt N.E. by N. and E by S: the riplinge contynuinge and current southerlie. Var: 18d. 11 minutes westerlie at sunne settinge.

6. Lat: 5d 5m waie S.E. by E. 18 leagues winde variable betwixt N.E. by N. and N.E. by E: a gale, and at sum times more fearfull riplinge of the water then before, yet could haue noe grounde at 100 fath. These riplinges shewe like shelves and are not at all times alike, but sume times more, sometimes lesse, but mett with manie times in a day, and make a noise by the shippes side as if shee did runne 5 leagues a watch, when shee doth scant got ahead. Wee were much terrified therewith, the rather because wee coulde not imagine from whence it should proceede, seinge noe land, but supposed our selues to be amongst the Easternmost Islandes which lie of the N.ermost pointe off St Laurence. Heere wee had rayne, thunder, lighteninge, and soden gustes which contynued not longe.

7. Waie E. by S. 18 leagues, winde betwixt the N. and N.E. the riplinge still contynued.

8. Way N.E. 22 leagues, winde at S.W. and S.W. by W. with riplinge but noe grounde at 100 fathum. Var: 20d. 7m westerlie.

9. Lat. 4d 18 minutes way N.E. 18 leagues winde variable, little current and noe riplinge. Var: 20d. 47m westerlie. Heere wee found it extreame hott.

10. Lat: 4d 12m waie E.N.E. 7 leagues, winde from N.W. by N. to N.E. by E. manie times calme with noe riplinge nor current southerlie. Nota wee haue found continuall calmes ever since wee came of the mayne, and the further of, the lesse winde. Variation 20d. 57 minutes westerlie.

                                               December 25.

1611   Doara

December 25 | Nota. It is a moneth and five daies, since wee were in Lat: 00. 01.m
to the N ward, close by the shoare, since which tyme wee haue bene put
They had passed | back into S⁰ 25 minutes to the southward. Wherefore those bounde to
the lyne a month | Socotora at this tyme of the yeare, must hould to the E. warde of Pemba
and 5 daies before. | 200 leagues, E. by N. the variation there increasinge westerlie, which will
bringe you the more northerlie. And soe keepinge the Island Socotora, open of
you, betweene the N by E. and the N. N. E. you shalbe in the greatest ∞∞
possibilitie to make the best vse of these windes, which neere to the mayne
wee founde to keepe betweene the E. by N. and E. by S. a contynuall gaole.
But of at sea, about the Islandes Mascarenas, at N. E. N. and sumetymes
at N. W: W. and W by S, with calmes riplinges of the water, were fearfull,
Thunder, and lightninge. And albeit the N. E. and northerlie windes
are but bare helpes plyinge to the N. wardes, yet this benefitt you shall
haue, that by howe much Easterlie you art, by soe much the more you shall
recover the northwarde of the lyne, before you meete with the mayne, W⁰⁰
if you can avoide see not in this tyme of the Easterlie Monson vntill you
be full in the Latitude of 10 degrees to the Northwardes of y⁰ Equinoctiall.
Nota. | But in the tyme of the westerlie Monson, keepe the shoare aboard, for it
is verie boult, but lieth much more Easterlie, then in our plattes.

January 1 | Latitude 3°. 58. minutes to the northward of the Equinoctiall. heere
wee made land, being the mayne of Magadoxa. Cape das Baxas, bearing
Magadoxo | N. N. E. 8 leagues of the land, lowe, sandie, and barren all alongest.
Cape das Baxas | The winde at N. E. and E. by N. a stiff gale, wee stoode of to the E. warde,
way N. by W. 12 leagues.

2 | Latitude 02°. 31. m. way S. E. by S. 35 leagues much winde and current
southerlie, havinge deprest the pole in these last 24 howers. 01d. 27. minutes
whereof 26 leagues, shee had runn by deade reckoninge, and 9. leagues shee
was carried by the currant contrarie to expectaron.

18 | Latitude 06°. 27. minutes, to the northwardes of the Equinoctiall, waie
N. W. by N. 24. leagues winde at N. E. and N. E. by E. About 2 of the
The mayne land | clock wee made the land, being the mayne called Doara, The south pte
called Doara | bearing W. and the N parte N. W. by N: about 8 leagues of, seeminge
not verie high but sandie and barren wee stoode of with much winde and a
Current setting N. W. as wee supposed, otherwise wee should haue gotten
further to the northward.

Nota that althought the variation houldeth little proportion, yet did wee
finde by experience that in runinge to the E. warde wee haue Variation
Westerlie increasinge. And standinge into the shoare N. W. our Variation
A notable thing | was Westerlie decreasinge, Soe that by reckoninge, according to our platte
concerning the | wee finde our selves much further of the land, then by iust proof by Var:
variation. | Which truelie is a most certen thinge to be credited. Observaron beinge
taken by one of experience, with an exact instrument. Our soe often fallinge
with this mayne hath gained vs this knowledge. Variation at sunne
rising 17°. 36. m westerlie, and setting 19°. 20. m. westerlie.

1611.   Zacotora.

February   1. The first daie wee made the land bearing N E by North about seaven
                leagues of, wee sounded and had grounde at 27. and 28 fathom, soft sand,
Cape Dorfuy   this land is called Cape dorfuy, being verie highe and barren, by the sea
                side, many gustes.

            9. Latitude 10d 37m wayt W by N 16 leagues winde N E by E, wee
                had now sight againe of Cape dorfuy, from whence wee departed the first
                daie contrarie to our expectation bearing N W about 9 leagues of,
                havinge founde a stronge current in the offing, setting W N W. which
                untill meetinge with this land againe, wee dreamed not of but rather
                thought wee had bene 45 or 50 leagues of, not once lookinge for the land:
                Wee sounded and had 50 fathum, fine smale sand, about 5 leagues of. This
                land is high and full of mountaines.

           10. Latitude 11d 20m way N E by E easterlie, 16 leagues winde from E by
Cape de Guarda N. to N E. wee sounded and had grounde at 45 fathom, smale black sand,
fui   about 8 leagues of the highe land of Cape Guardafuy, wee made triall of the
Abba dal Curia current with our pynnasse and founde it to sett N by E.
                Towardes eveninge wee had sight of the Island Abba dal Curia bearinge
                E N E. about 10 leagues of, being verie highe land, rising in two partes like
                two Islandes.

           14. Latitude 11d 32m winde N E. and E N E. calme. Heere wee had a sight
                of the Eastermost Irmana seeminge to the E ward, lowe landes about 6.
                leagues of.

           15. Latitude 11d 27m winde E S E. 6 leagues winde E: E N E: E S E:
                and N E. calme for the most parte, makinge attempt to be 8 leagues of
                the eastermost Irmana But wee were mistaken for it was Abba dal Curia
                and the duas Irmanas did beare N E of vs. 12 leagues of: Var: at sunne
                settinge 17d 23 minutes westerlie, and in the night the winde came faier,
                to the S S E, wee lay E with the stemme with help of a current to the
                Easterlie contrarie to the reportes of former navigantes. And by breake
Zacotora   of daie wee were 6 leagues of the W most Irmana bearing E S E. and
                had sight of Zacotora. 10 leagues of.

           16. Latitude 12d 19m. Variation at sunne risinge. 17d 22m. Westerly
                wee bare vpp and went about the wester pointe of Zacotora, towardes
                eveninge wee had sight of the white rock which lieth about 4 leagues of
                the westermost pointe of Zocatora the pointe and the rock bearinge one
                of thother N W by N and S E by S the said rock looming like a saile
                standinge to the E warde, larboarde tack aboard and was soe made for, by
                them of former voiages The current still helping vs to the E ward

           17. Latitude 12d 47m. Variation at sunne setting. 17 degrees. 22m. westerlie,
                winde variable at S E. and S E by S. calme but a stronge current setting
                alongest the land after wee were about the wester pointe.

                This night wee came to an anker one league and a halfe to the westward
                of the kinges Towne called Tamarin in 20 fathom water distant from
                the shoare 2 miles our shoalinge in, after wee had grounde was 22. 20. 19.
                20. 20. 20. smale white sand the winde E S E and S E. calme.

                                                                        18 feb:

1611.   Turkish trecheries.

February 18 — Wee came to an ancker in the roade of Tammarin, right before the
The rode of Tam- kinges howse in 9 fathum water, a league from the shoare, fine sandie
marin. grounde.

I sent mr Richard Cockes Cape marchaunt with the skiff, well appointed, vnto
the king to acquainte him what wee were and the cause of our cominge, and
to provide Cattell and fresh victuall. mr Cockes returned havinge byn
kindlie entertained and feasted by the king, and theise that went with him.
They brought a present of fresh victuall from the kinge Together with a
Letter left theire by Sir Henry Midleton dated the first of September 1611, &
aboarde the Trades increase in Delisha roade in the Ilande of Zacotora.
The originall I kept, and returned the coppie Verbatim, for the future
kepp'. Heere followeth the coppie.

   To the wor^{ll} and his verie good frindes, Generalles,
   Captaines, maisters, or anie other of the English or
   Dutch nation. &c.

Whosoeuer you are, that shall come
to the viewe of this premonition peruse it well and vse all diligence to
escape the danger hanginge over your heades; Wee giue you heereby to
vnderstand, That neither at Aden nor in Moha, nor in anie parte of the
Turkish tirannie in the Red sea, theire is anie trade for you: The Assension
which was to seeke trade first was greatelie iniured and wee of the 6.
voiage miserablie misvsed. Wee were intreated with all flatterinnge and
faire speeches that might be, with promise to be well vsed and profitted in
quiett trade. Wee deliuered our Presents for the Basha and performed
all kinde of duties, landed our goods, which were registred in y^e Custome=
howse, as wee thought in saffetie, wee had leaue to build our pynnasse on
shoare, soe purposing to settle our selues to trade and busied in buildinge
our pynnasse. Behould, what a wofull massacre happened on the 28 of
Nouember 1610, betweene 7 and 8 of the clock at night by comaundement
of the perfidcous Basha and trearkerous Gouernour of Moha wee were
by multitudes of armed souldiers assailed, 8 of our menn slaine out right,
14 wounded and the rest that escaped with life, beinge 51 persons, imprisoned
The Countrie and put in Irons both feett and handes. The cause was for cominge into
of yemen. this countrie of yemen (as the Turkes sayd) soe neere theire holy house. This
vsage beinge by the expresse comaunde of the greatt Turk, whoe hath
written to the Basha, That allthough hee should giue his licence to any
Christian to come hether, yet that heere they should staie theire shippes, &
kill theire menn and confiscate theire goodes. The same night that the
Massacre was committed there were 3 greatt boates, with above 100
souldiers sent aboord the Darling whoe did ride sumwhat neere the shoare, to
haue surprised her, but shee defended her self with the losse of 3 menn and
Sinan 14 daies 26 Turkes slaine. After our imprisonment heere in Moha, vntill the 22.
iorney vp into the of December 34 of vs, were carried to Sinan which is 14 daies iourney
conntry of Arabia. from

1611.   Turkish trecheries.

February.   18   from Moha, where wee were imprisoned againe, and the most parte of
                 vs clapt into waightie Irons, where at last coming to haue sentence of
                 the Basha, hee adiudged all the goods which wee had on shoare, with our
                 Pynnasse to be confiscate to the vse of the greate Turke, praising his
                 owne milde nature, that hee did not make vs captiues nor put vs to the
                 sworde, accompting it a greate good turne, that hee did lett our Persons
                 departe.

The sundrie trea-   As wee passed by Aden to come vnto Moha, the Governour was verie
sons of the Turks   desirous to haue one shipp left there (as they saide) to trade with them,
at Aden.   But theire purpose was to betraie her. But soe soone as two merchaunts
                     and the purser came on shoare they were staied, thinkinge by that meanes
                     to gett goods landed, demaunding to haue 1500 Chicquienes of Venice, for
                     ankoring or els to haue goods on land. In the meane time they practized
                     to cutt our Cables in the night, and other villanies. At length they
                     intercepted her boate with 17 men, which with the two merchaunts and
                     Purser, were likewise all sent vpp to Sinan with purpose to make vs all
                     Captiues, iff godd had not better provided for vs, Although to serue theire
                     owne turne, they sent vs all to Moha releasing 36 presentlie, and deteyninge
                     30 of the best on shoare vnder pretence of securing the Indian shipps
                     from the wronges which ours might offer them, But with purpose of
                     further mischeef towardes vs, from which wee (by the favour of God)
                     freed our selues by an escape, the 11t: of May 1611, otherwise (by reporte)
                     wee had bene deteyned heere captiues, or sent vnto Constantinople.

                     Iff yee be soe vnfortunate as to come into the Redd Sea, avoide the roade
                     of Moha, and the coast of Arabia, for there yee are to expect nothing but
                     treacherie.

The goodnes of ye   Yee shall vnderstand that vppon the Abesh shoare W by S. ½ pointe
roade of Asab—   Southerlie from Moha, there is a verie good roade, for all windes that doe
                     blowe in these partes called Asab Road, where yee maie haue woode and
                     water freelie and refreshinge for your money or course Callicoes, Iff wee
                     had not found this Roade, it would haue gone hard with vs our shipps,
                     ffor there is not gettinge out of this sea, from the middell of October,
                     vntill the middell of may, The windes contynueinge at S.E. and S.S.E.
                     Wee haue left diuers coppies of this advice at Moha and Zocotora. The
                     first that commeth to your handes recompence the bearer well, and make
                     vse heereof beinge thus warned by our harmes, And soe wee committ you
                     to the Lord who prosper vs proceedinges and deliuer you from your
                     ennimies. Written in Delisha roade, the first of September. 1611.

                     This following Postscript was written
                         with his owne hand.

                     You shall vnderstand that I arriued
                     heere the 28 of this present where I found kinde entertainment at
                     the Kinges handes and was frindlie vsed, having anie thinge I wanted
                     for my money Therefore I praie you whatsoeuer you be either of the
                     English or Dutch nation, to whome this present writing shall comme,
                                                                                    that

1611   Zacotora

February 18. that your demeanour bee good and kinde, and in soe doinge you cannot lack anie thinge the countrie yeeldeth. Vale. Chib. 3 August.

The king of Zacotora requested yt
our people comming for water might not spoile his date trees or greene Tobarro which to prevent, I gave strict commaundement to those whoe should from time to time be sent to the shoare.

19. I went on shoare accompanied with Capitaine Towerson, mr Corkes, all the marchaunts and a hundred muskateers commaunded by Capitaine Tobias Cocks, and at puttinge of ordered the Cloave to shoote 7 peeces, the Hector 5. and the Thomas 3. The king mett vs at the seaside. At our Landinge wee dischardged 50 of our smale shott, our Drummes beatinge and Trumpetts sondinge, the kinges musique aunswerringe them. The kinge ledd mee hand in hand vpp with him to his howse, where hee kindlie bidd vs welcome and feasted all the companie in verie royall manner, himselfe beinge richlie vested in Crimson velvett laide with with Gouldlace. His howse was built of Freestone Castell like, Hee had about 100 attendantes whereof about 50 went well apparailed accordinge to the Moorish fashion, the rest went naturalls of the Island. After manie complementes and curtesies, at night wee tooke our leaves of him, I commaunded two royalls of 8. to be given his musique whereof hee vnderstandinge would needes inforce vppon our Trumpettes. 4 Bookes of white callico, two peeces cottonee and one skynne of Dates. I presented the kinge with divers thinges at this present to the valiew of vmtlster. His name was Sultan Amur Bensaid. sonne to the king of Cushin vppon the Arab side. wee paide here for kyne 12 Royalls of 8 the peice, sheepe iijs the peice and for Goates one royall of 8. a peece which though it bee deere, yet are the moste of them not mans meate beinge soe vildlie and more then beastlie buggered and abused by the people as that it was most loath sum to see, when they were opened.

Wee paide for Rice iijd a pound, dates iijd a pound, hennes vijd a peece, & Tobarro 700 leaves a royall of 8: or 9s pence a peece. The kinge will take noe English money, but all Royalls of 8.

27. I caused a meetinge of the marchaundizinge Councell vnto whome I redd the Companies remembraunce, and the letter received by the handes of the kinge of Zacotora, from Sr Henrie Midleton, and shewed them, that whereas I had bene putt in good hope by the Companies remembraunce to have obtained good store of Aloes heere at Zacotora which nowe I founde frustrat the kinge beinge whollie vnprovided and not able to furnish vs therewith vntill August. And whereas wee were appointed to goe from hence to Aden and Moha in the redd sea, (the Monson not servinge for Surat) wee were nowe vtterlie disswaded from the viewe of those partes by the treatherous and wronge doinge to Sr Henrie and his fleete. And lastlie, whereas if wee did not goe for the redd sea, if wee should remaine heere in Delisha road 6 monethes, attendinge the monson, wee should finde it verie chargeable

The entertainem
of our Company
by the Prince of
Zacotora

or Caiexem

A.º 1611   Zocotora

February 27 chargeable and be able to effect nothinge, for untill the end of Septʳ. there is not cominge uppon the coast of Cambaia. My opinion was that notwithstandinge these badd tidinges receaved from Sʳ Henrie, yet that wee should goe for Moha, wee having with us the Graund Segniores passe, which the former shipps never had, ffor heere by wee should be able to certefie the companie, what steede the passe might stand them in, Determininge to stand uppon our Guard, and not to adventure anie one mann without good pledge: Soe that wee might ride securelie, and obtaine trade abourde, though none on shore, our forte beinge able to defend and offend uppon occasion the greatest power that port could raise. And findinge not hope of Comerce, then I entended to make use of his mats Comission in respect of the violence offred unto Sʳ Henry and his companie, and soe enforce the puttinge of of our English commodities or to make spoile of theire stale and Custome, by not permittinge the Indian shipps which were expected in the spur of March to enter there which would be a matter of not smale hindrannce unto them, but untill then I would be verie unwillinge to deale wᵗʰ them by force. And this course I did the rather approve of because there needd not partinge of companie, but the fleete might keepe together, and assoone as the Monson should permitt goe iointelie together for Zurat accordinge to the Companies order, there force united together, to resist whatsoever the enemie should attempt.

The Counsell utriwallie assented to what I propounded and soe concluded to keepe companie together, to goe for the redd sea.

29 I went on shoare and tooke leave of the kinge, hee promised mee yᵗ I should have his Aloes in the time of the yeere, but hee would not agree uppon anie price or quantitie.

The kinge requested mee to leave a letter with him to give those that should afterwardes come thether, to understand howe frindelie hee had delt with mee, which accordinglie I did, advisinge them with all of the price of victuall there, to the ende the countrie people should not cheat uppon them. ffor these Moores are verie understandinge and subtill.

March — 1 Wee waighed anckor and sett saile for the Redd sea, the winde at S. E. and S. sometimes little winde.

Nota, the winde since wee came to an anckor heere, went in the morninges and soe untill night for the most parte at N. E. by E. and E. N. E. and at night of the land betweene the S. and S. E. faire and temperate weather.

Nota goinge into the roade of Tammerin wee had these depthes as wee sounded, beinge verie good grounde, 17. 16½. 14. 13. 12. 11. 10. 9. 7¾. Then wee edged to the westwarde in the middle of the roade, under the highe homock to the Westwarde of the kinges Towne,

1611   Cape de Guarda fui

March 1. Towne which is built of freestone and shewed verie faire being flatt and whitt lymed, fronting before with the Castell which standeth uppon the topp of a smale hill upp in the land and had $7\frac{1}{2}$ 8. 8. 9. and $9\frac{3}{4}$ wee did lett fall our Anker a mile of the shoare, and going in with the towne, betweene vs and the shoare the fairer sholing afore it at a cast untill you come to 4 fathom: where wee might haue ridd a muskett shott of the shoare and further in 3 and $3\frac{1}{2}$ fathomb. It is Bold all the bay alongest keeping two Cables length of the land faier sand and some stones amongest. A demy Culveringe will reach the Castell, which is of noe force.

Latitude in Tammarin Bay 12º 35 minutes to the N. Variation 18 degrees 42 minutes westerlie. The kinge of Zacotora gaue me counsell that if I went to the redd sea I should plie to the southward of Abba del curia, for that keeping on the northside wee should be put ouer to the Arabian shoare and should not without greate troble fetch Cape Guardefui, soe that (by proof) wee found it best to keepe the Abash shoare aboarde.

4. In the morninge, wee sawe Cape Guardafui bearing W. 8 or 9 leagues of, wee steered in W.N.W. Latitude 12º 01 m the Cape S by W. 4 leagues of, noe grounde at 100 fathom the land high and smooth. Variation at sunne rising 17º 34 m westerlie. In the eveninge wee had grounde, standing in alongest the land, to finde the Baye of Feluke our depth was 26. 17. 18. 20. 21. fathom then noe grounde at 30 fathom then 32. 33. 31. 30. 30. 29. 28. 26. then being hard aboard the high homock called Mount Feluke wch lieth at the pointe of the lowe land of the nothermost part of the bay, off & Feluke and about two miles off seeinge noe daunger nor any suffe on the shoare although it was a lee shoare, and a prettie stiff gale wee stood of all night the winde at E. and S.E. And in the morning standing in, S.W. by W. our first grounde was 34. 33. 30. 28. 26. 24. 23. 20. 19. 17. 16. 15. 14. 13. 12. 11. 10. 9. 8. 7. 7. many casts 7. $8\frac{1}{2}$. 9. 10. 8. 9. $\frac{1}{2}$. 10. heere wee let fall our Anker, the mount or high pointe aforesaid bearing E.N.E. esterly $3\frac{2}{3}$ miles of, the lowe land stretchinge to sea to the westward of the homock N.E. by E. Easterlie 3 leagues. The westermost pointe which makes this Bay bearing W.S.W. $5\frac{1}{2}$ leagues off. The winde all daie N.E. a stiff gale, at night at E. and E. southerlie, the W. and W.S.W. then E. and soe continued betweene the E. and E.S.E. southerlie, distant from the neerest parte of the shoare a mile, fine white sand but noe fresh water to be had. Latitud 11º 53 minutes. Var: 15º 57 m westerlie. Distant from Cape Guardefui 16 leagues.

Heere wee resolved to goe for Moha and not to Aden because Aden is a towne of garrison and of little trade with other inconvenientes, as exaction of Custome &c as by the next voiage.

Heere wee tooke good store of Mulletts with our sayne, and other large & excellent fish with lynes and hookes.

Heere are Gumes of severall sortes verie sweete in burninge also fyne Matts well requested at Aden, Moha and the Indies. For ordinarilie the Indian shipps touch heere, both inward and outwarde, to buy thereof, and of the Gumes. Also victuall, sheepe, and butter which is farr better there then at Moha, for dailie boates got over laden with victuall to sell at Aden and

1611   Feluke.

March   4   and Moha, but they will not barter for any thing but lynnen cloth.
             Nota that at Feluke towne there is wood and water to be had plentie, but
The benefitt of   not in the bottome of the bay, the passage vpp to the towne is soe large, as
the towne of   that 3 shipps maie passe abrest without danger. The goinge in is betweene
Feluke.   the highe hom̄ork and the lowe sandie pointe.
             The maisters were willed to steere from hence W by N alongest the S: shoare
             to Demeti, and then to shape there course over to Aden.

         9   Latitude 11d. 58 minutes, way, W. 25 leagues, winde at E and E by S: a
             stiffe breese all daie, but at night little winde keepinge alongest the shoare
             some 8 leagues of. Wee steered W by N. Variation at sunne risinge 15 degrees
             10: minutes westerlie.

2 Smale Islands 10 In the morninge steeringe W by N the winde easterlie, wee had sight of two
                smale Islandes, lying of the highe land of Demety, about a league of the
                mayne distant from the other 4 leagues, the easternmost bearinge S. by. W
                7 leagues of and wee steered S. W the same distance, wee stoode over for the
                highe land of Aden N W by N. and N W, the winde at E and E by N
                a stiffe breese easterlie current. Var: 15d. 00 m. westerlie Lat. 11 58 m

         11 Wee had sight of the highe land of Arabia making it to be the highe land of
             Darsina bearing N by E. by the Compasse 8 leagues of. Latitude at
             noone 13d. 11m. Var. at sunne risinge 15d. 02 m westerlie, havinge had a stronge
             easterlie current coming over, for wee steered betweene the N N W and
             N. W, and went soe tarried to the E ward that shee hath made but a N by.
             W: way westerlie. But after wee were shott in about some 12 leagues of
             the shoare, wee founde no current, the pointe or headland of Aden breaking
             it of as wee supposed.

             I sent tenn instructions in writinge to Capten Cowerson and Mr Dawes
             to be observed at our arrivall in the roade of Moha, for the better grace and
             counteraunttinge of our action and safegardinge of our shipps, havinge to
             doe with soe treacherous a nation.

Var: 14 5 m W ly 12 Variation at Sunne risinge 14d. 5. minutes westerlie in sight of the highe
             land of Aden, bearing W by S: 10. leagues of, wee steered in W S. W. and at
             noone had Latitude 12 degrees 49 minutes, about 5 leagues of. The
             southmost pointe bearing S. W by S W, wee sounded and had grounde 18
             fathom, soft sand.

         13 In the eveninge 14 leagues to the E ward of the entraunte into the Straights
             and to the westward of Aden 16 leagues wee came to an anker, in respect
             wee were not acquainted with the coast, and findinge the inconveniences
             aforesaid, keepinge all daie within 3 or 4 leagues of the shoare, to the time
             wee Anckored, our soundinge was. 40. 38. 29. 18. 17. 16. 15. 16. 17. 16. 17. 19.
             18. 19. fathom, heere wee let fall our anker, sandie grounde the W. most
             land wee could see, bearing W by S: southerlie, and the highelande to the
             E ward N. N. E: about 4 or 5 leagues of.

         14 In the morninge wee weighed the winde at W by N, a smale gale with
             rayne, havinge had none vntill this present, those 4 monethes. Wee
                                                                              steered.

1611   Babel-mandel.

March 14 steered S.W by S. as neere as wee could lie for the straightes /
An the eveninge esteeminge our selues to be of the Straightes, wee shortened
saile, and stoode it of, and in, with a short saile keepinge our lead all night,
being 8. or 9. leagues of the mayne of Arabia, wee stoode of W by S. and had
not grounde at 100. fathom /

15. Our course W. by S. southerlie. 6 leagues winde E. S. E. The land which
on the 14 about 6 at night did beare W by S. 10 leagues of did nowe beare
S. W by S. 4 leagues of. To the E.ward theere wee had sight of 3 small Islands
or Homorks bearing N. N. W. ½ league. The greatest shewing, as if it
had a castell vppon it, beinge the E.most. Heere is a current setting from y
S. E. /from 6. in the morninge vntill 9. the winde at S. S. E. soe that wee could
stemme but S. W. The land which wee supposed to be the entraunce into the
Straightes (which at night did beare W. by S.) did nowe beare S. W by S.
soe that wee could not now wether it, having steered all night. W by S. /
The cause was, the current setting from the S. E. which put vs into the
Bay. But wee could set noe passage for theire was lowe land to the S.ward
of vs, which did beare S. S. W. of this supposed straight. And makinge a
hight land called Aspota, bearing N. E by. E. made vs suppose that this
was not the land entraunce into the Straightes, for the said highe land
of Aspota and the high land at the entraunce of the straightes doth beare
one from the other E by S. and W. by N. soe that wee could not bringe the
land S. W by S. as the supposed straightes did which proved this land to be
on the Abesh. shoare to the southward of the straightes of. Moha. And the
former Hummoks or Islandes to be to the W.warde of an Island in shape
like Penguin Island on our larboard side of the entraunce into the
straightes called Babel mandell, and having the winde at S. S. E. and the
supposed Islande Babel mandell. S. W by S, and the current setting S. E.
into the Baye, fleete weather, yet could wee perceaue noe passage /
Wherefore wee held to haue overshott it the last night to the W.ward
which proved not lesse. / For N. N. E. wee sawe two lowe Islandes 6. L
of, and a highe ragged land N E by N. 8 leagues of. The highe land
proved the head land, to the E. of the straightes and the lowe smooth Island
Babel mandell, the winde S. E. wee tackt to the N. ward and steered N. E.
and had 58 fathom 1½ league of the Island with the mount. And about
noone opened the straightes wee steered N. N. E. the winde at E. by S.
Then wee steered N and N by E. having 30. 38. 27. 28. 23. 21. 19. 18. 17. 15. 16.
10. 10. 12. 10. 9. 7. and 9. And when wee had opened the whithowse, which
standeth on a sandie bay, on the starboarde side of the entraunce N. E.
and the rock or lowe pointe on the same side. E. N. E. wee had 6. and 7 fathom
fyne black sand. Then wee steered N. N. E. vntill wee brought the rock or
lowe pointe E. ½ pointe southerlie, then N by W. Latitude at noone 12 d.
56. m. And keeping this course wee had 7. 6. 6¼. and as wee went in, the
deeper water. 14. 15 and. 16 fathum good ground, and at night did lett fall
our Anker in 15½ fathom black oze grounde. Distant from the Arabian
shoare. 3 leages, and from the Abesh. shoare on the other side 10 leagues
faire fleete wether, soe that wee could see from side to side, the winde at
S. S. E. little winde.

Aspota

Babel mandell

They could see from side to side of the straight

1611   The red sea.

March 16

The Shoale whereon the Trades Intreace struck

In the morne wee weyghed, the winde at E.S.E. wee steered N. by W. for Moha and had 18.16.15 fathom about 4 leagues the shoare Then wee steered N. and N. by E. and had 9. 10. 8 and 7 fathom, but findinge a shoale or banck which lieth to the S.ward of the towne, wee steered N.N.W. beinge in 8.9.7 fathom and edginge to the S.ward wee had 10. 11. 10½ untill wee brought the towne E. by S. southerlie of vs and were in 5½ fathom where wee let fall our anker. The steeple or high church standing in the towne bearinge E. and 1 league off, the pointe to the S.ward, S. by E. 3 leagues off.

Nota you must bringe the highe church E.N.E. Easterlie, before you shalbe cleered of the shoale aforesaid at your comming into the roade: which is verie dangerous and where the Trades Intreace did sett at least 24 howers and was fayne to the Companies greate losse to discharge a greate parte of her ladinge before shee gott of. But it shewed it self by the ruller of the water. Heere at entrie wee had verie much winde at S. and S.S.E. with a greate sea.

Not longe after wee went at Anker, the Governor sent vs a poore ould slave in a smale Canoo to knowe what was the cause of our comminge. I vsed the poore man kindelie, whoe of his owne accord tould me that the English that latelie were heere, were not well vsed by Regeb-aga, then Governour whervppon hee was cashiered, and that the Governo[r] at the present was called Ider aga a Grecian by birth, a man verie kinde to straungers and a greate frinde to merchaunts.

I willed the Purser to giue the poore man 2 Royalls of 8. and soe returned him to his Maister, with an swer that wee were Englishmen and frindes to the Grand Signior and would vppon his sendinge of a worthie and fitt man, acquainte him further with the cause of our comminge.

Presentlie after hee sent an Italian turned Moore, well clad with the like message to knowe whether wee had the Grand Signiors passe. I tould him I had not onelie such a passe, but likewise letters from the kinges Maiestie of Greate Britaine, vnto the Basha. The Italian desired to see them which I denied in respect I held him a base fellowe, from a Christian to turne Moore. But willed him to acquaint the Governo[r] therewith, and that wee were appointed in honor of the said passe, to shoote of 51 peeces of ordinaunte, at our arrivall heere in this roade, which I intended presentlie to doe.

The Italian intreated that hee might first giue his Maister to vnderstand thereof, which was graunted, and the purser willed to giue him 5 Royalls of 8. and his boate one. His name was Mustafa Trudgman.

The ordnaunce shott out of each shipp was. The Cloaue. 19. Hector. 17. Thomas. 15 peetes. The towne aunswered with. 5 peetes, ex[c]ellent Ordmaunce, and 2 Galleis 3 a peece These Galleis were stoute Galleis, of 25 Oares on a side and well fitted, yardes vpp. The Captaines name whereof was Mamee, and the Captaines name of the Towne was Mahumet bey.

1611.   Moha

March 17. I receaved a present from the Governour Ider aga viz: 3 Bullocks. 20
Hennes, two basketts of Plantens, and two of Lemmons with manie
complements, desiringe mee to come ashoare, I returned him a faier fowling
peece and willed the messenger to tell him that I desired to haue sufficient
pledge from him for my self, when I should come, for reasons not vnknowne
to the Governour. Geven to the messenger a redd cap, and a bottle of
wine which hee earnestlie craved, els should it not haue bene given him,
Doubting that if hee should be drunck therewith sume question might arise
to the hindraunce of our hoped for trade/

18. Wee waighed to goe neerer to the towne, the winde at S.S.W. vidmy to open
and muck winde, the maister was sent of to sound, whoe founde it bold. And
then Anckored in 5 fathom. The Church bearing E.S.E two miles of, and
the lowe pointe to the E: warde of the towne S:

The Governour sent his Secretarie vnto me, with a letter, to knowe what
annsweer I had formerlie returned him by Mustafa Trudgman, for hee
having gotten the bottell of wine was soe drunck therewith before hee gott
to the Governour as that hee could not speake. This letter was written
in Italian. Mr Corkes, and Bolton our Linguist, went sent ashoare to
acquaint the Governour that my cominge was to intreate trade, and
that whensoever it pleased him to send a man of equall worth to remayne
with the shipps as a pledge for my safe returne, I would in person come and
visitt him and alsoe to lett him vnderstand, that I was not ignoraunt of
the wronges donne by Regeb aga vnto Sr Henry Midleton my
Countrieman and his companie/. But if wee might now haue quiett
trade, all matters passed should be forgotten and wee would treate with
him of such our busines, as the Grand Signior had given vs leave, which I
hoped should be for all our goode/

The Secretarie remained aboarde pledge for mr Corkes and Bolton, and hee
did eate our vittualls, but had it drest by his owne people/

At night they returned, having byn well vsed, feasted vested in cloth of silver
and carried vpp and downe the towne with musique before them, to give
the people to vnderstand howe welcome they were, as Mr Corke vnderstood it,
But contrarie to expectation or custome (as wee can learne) at theire
coming away to returne aboarde, they were brought into a howse, and
disrobed of theire vests/. I asked of the Secretarie whether it were ordinary
and vsuall with them soe to doe, hee aunswered yes. I replied that in noe
other parte of Turky the like was donne that ever I heard of. In the end the
Secretarie was dismissed, and halfa a violett kersey given him, hee was very
importunate to knowe whether I were not of kinde vnto Sr Henrie
Middleton, the like was demaunded of Mr Corke by them ashoare, fearinge
that I was come to take revenge of them/

Nota   Wee supposed that the reason which moved the Governour to be soe desirous to
haue me come ashoare was, that the factors and Ledgers for the East Indian
marchaunts, that lye heere might give intertaynement to the Indian shipps
(which dailie were expected) to come in heere, for the advaunce of theire
skale and custome, which otherwise they feared would goe vp to Judda and
other ports, if they did heare of our being heere, and of the iniuries donne to
the

1611.   Moha

March   18 the English the last yeare/ But I resolved not to goe ashoare with-
             out pledge nor to departe without puttinge our english commodities
             in barter for Indian goods, at the cominge in of the shipps/ The
             secretarie at partinge intreated to haue some peeces of Ordinaunce
             given him for his credit which was graunted, 3 shott out of the Cloave
             and one peece out of the other two shipps/

         19 Captaine Mamee Captaine of the Gallies, sent me a Present of hens
             and Chickins, with a letter, shewinge that the Aga would send the
             theefest person next himself to remayne aboarde, if I would come a
             shoare, I accepted thereof, and sent worde, that shortlie I would
             visitt him/

         20 The Governour sent aboarde Mahumet Aga Admirall of the shoare
             and commaunder of the Roade, for the Turkes custome and Anckorage,
             and Nasuffe a graue ould man with two attendants proper menn,
             to remaine pledged for me, Soe I went ashoare with all the
Our Landing marchaunts the three skiffs well fitted and had 51 peeces of ordinaunce
at Moha   shott out of the shipps at partinge/ I was receaved at the landinge
             place by the captaine of the Gallies, and divers other principall menn
             with waites, Drumes and other musicall instruments playinge
             before, and divers peeces shott out of the Castell/ The people followinge
             in such aboundaunce that wee could hardlie passe/

             havinge passed two Guardes of verie proper men well cladd wee were
             brought into the Governors howse, which is built all of freestone,
             with verie faire and large staiers, and soe were ledd into a roome,
             spredd with rich Carpetts/ At the upper end of the roome was a
             windowe made after the fashion of our Baye windowes where a
             Silke Quilt was spredd vppon the floore, and two Cushions of
             Cloth of silver laide thereon/

             I was requested to sitt downe, but presentlie the Governor came forth
             of another chamber accompanied with 5 or 6 persons richlie apparelled
             himself in a gowne of Cloth of silver faced with rich furre/ Hee tooke
             mee by the hand kist his owne hand and putt it to his head/ Then hee
             ledd me by the hand to the said windowe where wee satt downe, And
             after some fewe complements, I delivered vnto the Governour our
             kinges letter, which mr Corkes did reade and Bolton our linguist
             interpreted to the Captaine of the Gallies, and hee to the Aga, which
             course hee held for state/

             After I delivered him the Grand Segniors Passe which hee gave to his
             Secretarie to reade which donne hee tooke it, kist it, and laide it vppon
             his heade without further ceremonie/

             The coppie of the said Passe followeth in these wordes/
                      viz./
                                                                    Hee that are &c

1611
March 20

The Turkes passe

Yee that are my most lawdable fortunate, wealthie and greate Vice reys Beglerbeys, that are on the waie from my most happie and Imperiall Throne (both by sea and land) vnto the confines and Boundes of the East Indies, Owners of some parte of dignitie, and those vnto whome belongeth to giue aide help and succour in Gods cause, and Mussulmanicall Religion, vppon theire Emperours beck, The wealth and greatnes of whome, lett it contynewe forever / Likewise vnto yee my most lawdable and valiant Saniacgbeys, that are vnder the aboue named Beglerbeys owneres of hope of future greate dignities, and those vnto whome belongeth dutifull aide and help in Gods cause and religion vppon theire Empero's direction, the honor and dignitie of whome be ever continuinge / And vnto yee my most lawdable wise and prudent Iustices of peace, Iudges and ministers of Iustice that are within the precinctes of the saide Saniacgheys whose Iudgementes, Iustice and wordes, doe flowe as from a fountaine of all wisdomm and prudence, The worthines and greatnes of whose dignitie and function, lett it continewe forever /. Allsoe vnto yee my lawdable, greate and most worthy Captaines and Reyses of all our Nauies and shippinge, that swimme vppon the face of the sea, vnto yee my lawdable captaines of the Castles, citties, and townes, And vnto yee worthie and Lawdable Customers dwellinge vppon the sea coaste, vppon Riuers, Bridges, and all other partes of our Dominions, and therevnto adiacent / vppon sight of this my most highe and Imperiall comaundement in conformitie of yo' most bownden duties you shall arise and doe obey saunce and reverence therevnto / Heereby yee shall vnderstand that the Embassado' of the kinge of greate Brittayne, that resideth in our happie and most high porte, hath giuen vs to vnderstand by his supplication That forasmuch as some of his maisters the kinge of greate Brittaines his subiectes haue with greate charge and labour discouered a trade in the East Indies, and withall vnderstand of wealth and likelihoodes of trade in some partes of o' Dominions by the waie to be had in the way to the passage to the East Indies, Beinge therefore desierous to visitt those places for the better inlarginge of theire said trade, to th'end that such men in soe good and lawdable enterprises, haue all fauour aide, and help, soe farre as lawfullie and convenientlie maie be graunted, hath requested vs in the name of his said maister the kinge of greate Brittame to vouthsafe them our safe conduct and recommendations / In conformitie of whose request as alsoe in regarde, wee and our predecessors are, and haue byn for the space of many yeares in strict league and amitie with the aforementioned king of greate Brittaine and the subiects of that kingdome, whoe longe haue had, and at this present haue

free

free traffique and trade in merchaundizinge in our Dominions and
Provinces through the Mediterarrean Seas. Wee therefore doe
commaund and expresslie charge you all and everie one of yee our
about mentioned subiects and officers that yee will not onelie kindlie
and lovinglie entertaine and receaue the said marchaunts and subiects
of Greate Brittaine cominge or passinge throughe or by any of our
Dominions, especiallie intendinge to trade to the Dominions of
yee yemen, Aden and Moha and the partes adioyninge therevnto
Assistinge and relieuinge them with all thinges needefull for
themselues theire men and shipps. But alsoe freelie to permitt them
by land or by sea to goe or saile outwardes and returninge even as
theire occasions shall require and to remayne in anie of our
Dominions countries or citties, grauntinge them such libertie of
traffique and priviledges as shalbe reasonable without giuinge or
sufferinge anie lett or hindraunce Iniurie or molestation to be
offred or donne vnto them; yea yee shall yeeld vnto them such offices
of Beneuolence and humanitie as shalbe meete and convenient to
be yeelded vnto honest menn and strangers vndertakinge soe longe
and laborious a voiage. And if soe be that wee shall vnderstand
that contrarie to the Capitulations the Amitie and league which
is betweene vs and the kinge of Greate Brittaine yee doe offer them
the least wronge and anie waie molest and troble the said merchants
in theire traffique and ought els. Knowe yee for certaine, that yee
shall not onelie incurr our high displeasure but yee shalbe punished
for example vnto others. And therefore carrie your selues conformable
to this my Imperiall Ensigne. Written at our mansion Guarde
at Constantinople on the thirteenth daie of the moone called zilkigie.
Anno 1019.

Hee told me that I was welcome, desiring

that what was formerlie past touchinge Sir Henry Middleton
might not be remembred, for that the quarrell grewe by two
dronken men and was by the then Gouernour rashlie followed, for
which hee was displaced 5 monethes since. And as concerninge
trade hee could not permitt anie greate matter till hee had direction
from his maister Jafar Basha of Sinan, whome hee had written
vnto and would with 10 or 12 daies returne an aunswer. Earnestly
intreatinge mee that I would permitt my people to com on shoare to
buy what they wanted and to sell smale matters to the end that the
naturalls might see that wee were in peace and amitie together and
that what was past was forgotten. These his speiches made good
what I had formerlie contained, touchinge the doubt that the East
Indian

1611 Moha.

March 20. Indian shipps would make of theire cominge in heere, unles they understoode, that wee were all frindes, and theire not cominge in here would
be a greate hindraunce to everie officer of this Porte. Besides wee
riddinge sot neere the shoare (as wee did of purpose) as that not laden shee
could come in, but that shee must perforce ride within call of us, which
did put them in the greater feare, whereby I resolued my selfe suer of
trade either ashoare, or aboarde the shipps, and that keepinge the towne in
this awe, I might the more bouldlie adventure my skiff and people
to the shoare to fetch what our shipps wanted.

The Governour feasted mee and the rest of us verie roiallie at a dinner
with all sortes of wilde foule, Hennes, Goates, mutton Creame, Custardes
divers made dishes, and Confections all served in vessells of tynne, (&
different from our pewter) and made Goblett fashion with feete. The
dishes sot placed the one uppon the other that they did reach a yard highe,
as wee satt, and yet each dish readie to be delt uppon without remove.
The meate was all served upp at once, and that before wee sate downe.
Our drinke was water simplie, or els water boiled with an hearbe
called Cau haw therein which is in tast somewhat bitter. Wee did sitt
crosse legged uppon Carpetts laied uppon the floore, for there they used
neither Tables nor stooles.

Dynner ended, hee ledd mee into an Inner chamber, where hee had fower
little boies that attended him beinge his boyes of pleasure, there wee two
beinge sett uppon a crimson velvett carpett, the rest of the chamber floore
beinge spredd with verie ritch Carpetts, one of the boies, bearing a lynnen
napkin in his hand did usher in two of the other, whereof the first had a
silver Chafingdish with coales, The other brought a dish wherein were
divers ritch perfumes. Vizt Amber greece, Lignum Aloes, and others.
The Governour requested mee to lett the boye cover my heade close with
the napkin which donne, the other boy held the chafingt dish under my
heade, that I might receave the fume which was verie pleasant.
After I had finished The Governour, and two other chefest menn about him
did the like, beinge (as it seemeth) a Cerimonie much used amounge them.
Havinge conferred a while together, there came in three of the boies againe
the one brought a vest or Gowne of Cloth of Goulde, wrapped upp in a
case of Taffetie died in saffron to preserve the cullour of the Gould.
The other boy had a Shash or Turbant, striped all with gould, and in
length 22 yardes. The third, a Damaskeene or Turkish sworde,
ritchlie garnished with silver and guilt both hilt and scabbard.
The Governor himselfe did put the vest uppon mee, and did girte the
Damaskeene unto my side, tellinge mee that they were not presents from
himselfe, but commaunded by the Grand Signior who (as hee said) did
bestowe them uppon mee; And in treated mee to ride with the Cady (who
is cheef Justice there) and the Captaine of the Gallies about the towne,
that the people might take notice of the amitie and frindshipp that was
betwixt us.

They

1611   Moha.

March – 20 They brought a horse richlie trapped, the mettell worke of the bridell all of silver, But I rather chose to goe on foote, that I might the better viewe the towne, whereunto they gaue consent. And soe wee walked together about the towne. And hauing viewed a howse wherein to haue setled our Ffactorie, I was brought to the howse of the Captaine of the Gallies, where I had a costlie banckett. And then returninge by the Governours howse, hee mett me vppon the staires, where agayne earnestlie intreatinge, that the discourtesies offred S.r Henry Midleton might be forgotten, and that it might appeare by my often comminge or sendinge my people ashoare, wee tooke our leaues one of another. And soe accompanied with a greate trayne of the best of the towne, I returned aboarde, where the shipps discharged 15 peeces of Ordinance. The Turkes that remained Pledges, hauing diuers Presents given them, were sent frindelie ashoare, and had 15 peeces shott of at theire partinge.

21. I sent m.r Corkes and others ashoare with a present to the Governo.r a case of Bottells filled with Rosa solis, which hee did earnestlie desire me to giue him, and to send it soe wrapped vpp as that it might not be knowne what it was. Likewise was sent two pecce of Violett Broadecloth to his Eunuches. They had further direccons given them to inquire ashoare what customes were due in and out. The waightes, measures, & valuation of Coines, prices of Indicoes, Callicoes, Cotten yarne, and other commodities fitt for vs to lade. Also to procure the Iewe to come aboarde whoe was in the Assension at her castinge away neere y.e Barr of Suratt, and could giue vs certen intelligence of Sir Henries successe, &c.

This night late the winde blowinge verie stiff, soe that o.r longe boate could not come from the shoare the Governour commaunded two greate Telbaes of his to hale her to windeward of the shipps and towe her aboard, ffor which curtesie, his men were rewarded and thanckes returned to the Governour whoe doubtles by this, shewed howe willing hee was to prevent all disorders and brables, which might arise by our mens being ashoare, in the night time.

The Governour did nowe request the Grand Sigmors Passe that hee might take a coppie thereof, which donne, hee returned it againe.

Nota:— That this roade of Moha, is verie open and dangerous with verie shoale water a mile of the towne, lowe land even with the sea. At this present the winde S. S. W. a greate storme, which caused such a sea as that wee did send not lesse then 7 feett ridinge in 5 fathom. And the winde at W. you haue not succour but the countrie people saie, that in the time of those

Extremitie of heate beginnge in the fine of May.
windes which beginn in the fine of May, the extremitie of heate is such as that it deades the winde, which makes that season verie contagious.

22. The Capitaine of the Gallies sent mee Present vz.t a sallett of Lettice, and a Iarre of milke sealed vpp, and manie complements and willed M.r
                                                                                              Corke

1611   Moha

March 22 — Cockes to tell me that it was fittinge for mee to hier a howse ashoare in time before the Indian shipps came in, for that then they would be deere, and fewe or none to be hadd, and that wee could not haue a faier howse vnder 100 Royalls of 8, for the Monson, thone halfe to be paide before hand.

23 — The Aga sent of a boate to knowe if wee wanted anie thing and to bringe suth of our people on shoare as I pleased to send, the weather soe exceedinge fowle, as that our boates could not budge. The winde at S. and by W.

I writt vnto the Aga, and the Captaine of the shoare, thankinge them for theire curtesie in sendinge soe to me, and shewinge that the reason that none of our people came ashoare yesterdaie was because it was our Sabaoth, on which daie wee are not to labour but to keepe it holie, and serve God.

24 25 — The weather continued soe fowle, as that wee could not send a shoare, nor any Boate come of to vs.

1612

26 — The skiff was sent ashoare with m^r Cockes to inquire if aunswer were come from the Grand Basha. In the eveninge hee returned, bringinge good store of fresh victuall that hee had bought, but not newes yet from the Basha.

28 — I receaued a letter which was left heere by m^r Laurence Femell cape marchant of the trade, in Aprill 1611 beinge the coppie of the letter which Sr H. Henrie left with the kinge of Sacatora. I receaued it from one Hosoroofe whoe requested it might be kept verie secrett, because it concerned his life. I recompenced him well, and gaue him the letter againe to deliuer vnto anie that shoulde heereafter come, vnderwritinge therein, that it had formerlie by me byn perused.

31 — I vnderstoode from the captaine of the towne that yesternight late arived the messenger from the Grand Basha with letters to the Governour to this effect: That hee should yeeld vs peaceable trade, both on the shoare and with the Indian shipps as hee would aunswer the contrarie at his perill And to lett vs furnish our selues with what wee wanted. I was doubtfull of the certentie of this pleasinge newes for that not halfe an hower before, m^r Cockes had speech with the Gouernour whoe spake of no such matter. The Capitaine said that the reason of the Governo^{rs} not speakinge thereof, was because there was a Gelba bounde for Mecca and readie to departe which he would not haue to knowe, that the Basha had graunted vs trade, fearing least they should acquainte the Shriff at Mecca therewith, whoe by his letters to the Grand Signior might cause the Graunt to be revoked. But wee rather think the Basha hath returned some harsh aunswer with direction to doe that vnto vs, which as yet hee cannot effect, wee beinge soe wrathfull and warie ouer him. And therefore will not be knowne to haue receaued aunswer from Sinan, till better bethinking.

Nota: Nota. Hosoroofe, hee that sent m^r Ffemales lre did nowe send worde by our lmguist, that I should beware of cominge ashoare my self vnles I had good Pledge, as formerlie, and then I might bouldlie come but otherwise not to trust them, though the gouernour should sweare vpon his Alcaron.

                                                                             for

1612   Moha.

Aprill   1   ffor they were souldiers and did not much respect oathes, And as hee
             heard, the newes that was come from the Basha, did not tend to our
             benefitt, for that the coppie of the Grand Signiors Passe, was not as
             then come to the Bashaes handes. But then should be fullie seene
             what would be doune, which would be within 6 daies.

         2   This daie the Caravan from Grand Cairo in Egipt, arived heere in
             Moha.

         3   This daie came into the Roade two Indian shipps one of Chaul, the
             other of Cananor. Theire ladinge Indicoes, Calicoes, Pintadoes, Amber-
             greece and Cotton yarne, with at least 400 passengers, whoe carried
             much wealth about them. Wee saluted them with 9 peeces of ordinance
             out of our fleete, they aunswered with 3 Chambers apeece, being all
             they had. I sent my skiff, to inquire what newes vppon the coast of
             Surat. The Captaine sent worde, that there were three English shipps
             tradinge there, but further could not tell.

             The Captaine of the towne with five cheef Janisaries, came aboard
             being sent by the Governour, to lett me vnderstand, that the Basha had
             written vnto him, to intreate and vse vs kindelie, and to permitt vs
             peaceable trade, desiring me, that I would in person come on shoare y
             next morninge and I could further vnderstand. I craved pardon, not
             forgettinge Hosoroofes admonition, But Captaine Towerson, beinge
             desirous to goe ashoare, the Captaine was requested to tell the
             Governour, that I vppon good Pledge would the next morninge send my
             brother vnto him, which was well liked of. Soe havinge feasted the
             Captaine and his retinewe, and given them divers Presents, they were
             sent ashoare with 21 peeces of ordinaunce at partinge, which hee sent
             worde that hee tooke soe well as that wee should not want the best
             assistaunce hee could doe vs.

         4   In the morninge, though the Pledges, were not yet come, yet desirous to
             see what the Basha had ordred Captaine Towerson was sent ashoare
             for wee helds the two Indian shipps, which rodd hard by vs, for sufficient
             Pledge if on shoare anie iniurie should be offred. The Governour vsed
             him frindlie and vested him to content, but nothing was effected of that
             hee went about. The Turkes not performinge theire promise.

             The Governour sent worde that it would be fittinge to send two of our
             menn of good fashion vpp to the Basha to Sinan, with the kinges letter
             and Present and then speedie dispatch would be had to our likinge.
             whereof I approved, intendinge the next daie, to laie out a Present for
             him.

3 letters from
Captaine Midleton   5   The captaine of the Gallies sent me 3 letters which the last night came
and Capt. Sharpeigh   to the Governors handes from Sir Henry Midleton and Captaine
                        Sharpeigh whoe ridd then at an Anker at Babel mandel. The effect
                        whereof was to lett me vnderstand, That he was come from Surat and
                        had little or noe trade there, That Captaine Hawkins vppon distast was
                        come from Agra and with his wife, was aboarde his Shipp. That hee
                                                                                    had

1612   Moha

Aprill 5   had brought all awaie from thence except one mann of Captaine Hawkins
which went over land for England, and that hee was come back to bee
revenged of the Turkes wishinge mee therefore to gett my Goodes and
people aboarde with all speede.

Hereuppon, I altered what yesternight was agreed uppon, and forthwith
sent one of the marchantes awaie to Sir Henrie with a Letter The effect whereof
was, to lett him understand of the proceedinges of our voiage, and of the mann
of our entertainement heere hetherto. That if hee had not thus come in, I had
on Mundaie sent two men of fashion upp to Sinan. But nowe uppon
Conference with him doubt not but that some course maie be resolved uppon
to the better advauncement of both voiages.

Nota   The two Indian shipps aforesaid, did discharge heere these Goods followinge
Viz. Lignum Aloes. 60 kintalls, Indico 600 Churles, out of both shipps
Shashes of all sortes, greate store, Sinamon of Selon. 150 Bahars, each Bahar
3 1/2 Churles, Offer (which is a redd dye) greate quantitie, Cloues greate store,
Bastas or whit Calicoes from 20 Rialls of 8 the Corge to 40 Royalls a
Corge (beinge 20 peeces) a greate quantitie, the price of Indico was from 30
to 35. 40 and 50 Royalls of 8 the Churle.

6   I writt unto the Captaine of the Gallies, onelie to continewe frendshipp, whoe
returned a friendelie letter unto me.

7   I writt unto the Captaine of the towne that hee should procure the Indian
Marchauntes to barter with me at reasonable rates for such of theire comodities
as I should desire, and as might serue to lade one of our shipps, which doinge
would satisfie Sir Henrie of theire nowe frendlie meaninge towardes us and
cause him to forbeare all Hostile attempts &c. Att this present, there
was a greate rumor spredd in the towne, of a Felba or two which Sir Henry
had taken, cominge over from the Abesh side, with virtuall. In respect
whereof, wee durst scarcelie adventure our Skiff and Ging ashoare.

I receaved a letter from Sir Henrie by a Felba which hee had taken at the
Bab, The effect was, as his former, To disswade me from tradinge heere.
I receaved an other letter from Captaine Mamee that the annswer which the
Governour had receaved from the Basha, was in these wordes viz.

Ider aga, you haue writt me, that three

English shipps are comme to Moha to trade in marchaundize with the
Grand Signiors Passe Give them faithfull promise from me to come ashoare
to take a howse untill the Monson be past, to buy and sell. You haue likewise
written mee that they will send upp two menn unto me. Give them all
thinges fitt for theire Journey. Captaine Mamee did further writt that
what I would propounde the Aga, and hee would underwrite. That for
Barteringe, they would doe somethinge for love but nothinge by force, and
were as willinge to lade all the three shipps, as one.

Nota   As wee were informed, the weight heere used is called an Jnen, which is
two Rottallas. A Rottalla is a pounde of theire weight.

                                                                            10 Jnens

1612.   Moha

Aprill .. 7. Tenn Juens is 20 pounde of theires, which make 23 poundes
            English, Haberdepoiz sometymes 24 poundes as the water will
            befrinde you / A Churle of Indico by theire weight is tos 150lb and
            of ours betwyxt 166. and 170 pounde / Cotten Wooll is sould by the
            Bahar which is 300 Rottallas makyng betwyxt 332 and 344 pounde
            English, at 18 Royalls of 8 the Bahar, verie good and cleane / Theire
            measure of length is called a Peeke, contayning 27 Inches or three
            quarters of our English yarde /

         9. The Governour sent of a Canoo, to intreate me, that in the mornynge
            I would send ashore, and I should haue both the Bashaes aunswer, and
            a warrant to staie all such Junckes as shall passe Sir Henrie, and
            force them to come in hether, and trade with them for such of theire
            Goodes as I desired, &c. And that I would suffer my people to come
            ashore, because the marchauntts were nowe growne fearefull by reason
            of Sir Henries displeasure /

        10. Mr Corke was sent ashoare and had conference with the Governo[ur] and
            Captaine Mamee whoe tould him that they were nowe fullie resolved,
            that what they had formerlie promised, they might not performe, The
            Cady dysliking thereof, sayng that they might hazard theire owne lives
            thereby, That neither marchaunt nor Broker would come aborde as
            I had requested, the knight had soe discontented them, That they of Grand
            Cairo had theire ffactors there which lay purposelie to ingrosse Indicoes
            and other Indian comodities whereof they would not buy vntill they
            should see what quantitie would come / That the Banians or Indian
            Ladyers ashoare, which haue Indicoes in theire handes would not sell,
            hopyng of a scarcitie / Hee alsoe brought woorde, that they deny asshore
            to buy any of our Goodes vnles wee will land them first /

  Nota   The Grand Signiors Customes of this Porte Moha is worth yearlie vnto
            him 150000 Chicquenes which rated at   shillinges sterling p peece,
            is   poundes sterling / Accordinge to the Reporte of the
            Governour to mr Corke /

        11. I caused the marchandizyng councell to meete and consult what was
            best to be donne, seeing that Sir Henry thus kept the Junckes from
            commyng hether, and that there was then noe further hope of trade
            heere / It was agreed vppon that vntill the Monson would permitt
            vs to proceede further wee should continewe frindshipp with the towne
            as hetherto wee hadd donne /

        12. I beeing informed of Sir Henries earnest desire to speake with me and
            protestations of greate kindnes and love towardes mee, resolved to
            goe vnto him, and soe willed the maister with the first winde to sett
            Sale for Babel Mandel, whereof I did lett the Governour of the
            towne to vnderstand, and tooke a letter of his to carrie to Sir Henry
            the better to continewe frindeshipp still with him /

                                                                        13.

1612.   Moha.

April 13   About 6 at night wee sett saile for the Bab, wee steered S and by
             W, the winde at N and N and by W.

       14   In the morninge wee arived at the Bab, where wee founde the Trade
            Increase riding, and 4 Indian Junckes or shipps. I went aboarde the
            Trade where I remained untill night, but nothinge could at that
            tyme be conclueded betwixt us.

       15   Sir Henry came aboard the Clove.

       16   Seinge Sir Henries resolution called my Councell together, and
            acquainted them with what I observed thereuppon, and that in regarde
            that by these Iarrs happened betwixt Sir Henrie the Turkes and the
            Cambayans, our hopes of anie trade to be had at Suratt was as smale
            as that which wee hadd alreadie founde at Moha. Our best course
            would be that the Hector and Thomas should waigh Anckor and ply
            betwene Aden and the Babb. The Cloave to keepe the Abesh Channell
            there, that none might passe by in the night, And soe to meete with as
            manie of the Indian shipps as wee could, to whome wee might put off
            our Broade cloth, Leade, Tynne, Iron, and Elophants teeth, commodities
            which were provided for those parts, in Barter for such as I knewe would
            vent well in these countries. Whether wee went afterwardes to goe.
            If wee lighted uppon Inditoes, they would be good for England. Also ye
            I had certen intelligence of two verie greate shipps dailie expected called
            the Rehmi, and the Hasani, the least of them (by reporte) able to lade the
            Hector with requestable commodities. Heerunto they generallie assented,
            to be putt in practize, with the first winde.

       17   I went aboarde the Trade where at length this agreement was made,
            That both fleetes should ioyne to trade with as manie of the Indian shipps
            as they could meete with, and to exchange our English commodities with
            them for theirs.
            Sir Henrie to dispose of two thirde parts of all the Goodes which should be
            bartred for, from this daie forwardes, And the other thirde, the Grand Sigmor
            to haue his Customes paide. Heereof writinges were made beinge sealed
            and delivered betwixt us. The Hector and Thomas were appointed to
            plie betwene the N: end of Babel Mandell and the Abesh shoare, to
            meete with all such as should come that waie, With charge that noe
            mann should take the value of one penne out of them, or offer the least
            violence to anie of their persons.

       18   In the Eveninge of Cananor arived, laden with Spice, Druggs, and
            other commodities, I sett saile for Moha, the winde at S and S and by E
            a stiff gale, where wee arived within 5 howers after. The Governour
            presentlie sent off to me, intreating to knowe howe all thinges past at the
            Bab, requestinge that my linguist might be sent ashoare to acquainte him
            therewith.

       20   The Skiff was sent ashoare to fetch our linguist, whoe returned, and brought
            a Present of fresh victualls from the Governour to me.

                                                                              The

*My returninge to
Moha was in hope
of dealing for 1000
Churles of Indico
which I was promi=
=sed.*

1612.   Moha.

Aprill. 20 The Skiff was fitted, and m.r Corkes sent ashoare in her, with a muster of
             our Commodities which the Governour intreated to haue presentlie sent
             him, Hee liked of divers rullers of our Broade cloth promising to take for
             1000 Royalls of 8. besides some quantitie of Tynne and Lead, manie others
             desired to haue Leade and Iron, Wherefore hee intreated that in the morning
             some quantitie thereof might be brought ashoare, for hee having once
             begun the marchaunts would certenlie followe and trade with me,
             Hee sent three examples of Indico but none of Lahor which is rounde and
             the best, The price 100 Royalls of 8. the Churle, which is 127 pounde
             or Rottallaes of Moha, and about 150 pounde English, but they would not
             sell by anie other waight, then that they bought by which they might very
             well doe, the price soe vnreasonable, for wee esteemed the three sortes to be
             worth but 30. 40. and 45 the best the Churle /
             I writt to Sir Henry and Captaine Towerson and sent my letters overland
             by Mahumudd Secretarie to the Gallies /

         21 I sent ashoare 8 Clothes one Tunne of Iron, 1 Tunne of Leade, two Chests
             of Tynne, They offred for 4 of the best clothes, 3 and ½ royalls the Peece which
             should be 27 Fnithes, but measured by another Peeke proved to be 31. in the
             The Bahare of Tynne 120 Royalls, The Bahar Iron 12 Royalls. And
             Lead 15. Royalls of 8. which were not pritis to our likinge, soe as might ye
             merchaunts it turned with theire Commodities aboard againe /

         24 m.r Corkes was appointed to goe to the Bab overland but beinge on shoare,
             a Ielba came aboard with letters from Sir Henry and Captaine Towerson,
             By reason whereof a signe was made to call him aboarde againe /
             In these lres, Captaine Towerson gaue mee to vnderstand of the mutenny
             of his Companie, and of the arrivall of two greatt shipps, And that S.r
             Henry and hee were minded to goe for Assab roade /

         25 Vppon conference with m.r Corkes, I resolved to sett saile and goe to Assab
             where wee came to an Anker the 27. about 8 of the clock at night and
             founde the Trade and Hector ridinge there, with 11 saile of Juncks, or
             Indian shipps of severall places /

Nota.   Nota. That comming into this roade or Harbor keepe the Northeren side
             aboarde leavinge a little rock or Hummok on your Starboard side then
             wee had 12. 11. 10. 9. 8. and 7 fathomes, sandie grounde, and in 7 fathom wee
             let fall our Anker about half a mile of the shoare /

         28 Captaine Towerson brought divers of the Mutenets aboarde the Cloave,
             some others denyinge to come, soe that I was inforced to goe aboarde the
             Hector to reduce that distracted Companie into some better order which
             with some troble was at last effected, The maister removed and another
             put in his place /

         30 I sent my Skiff to the Juncks to giue warninge to the Kohodaies and
             Marchaunts, that they should not offer to sett saile without my leave, The
             Kohodaies and principall of them requested that such of theire Goods as
             wee desired might be sorted out of hand, that they might not loose theire
                                                                           Monson

1612.   Moha.

Aprill. 30 Monson of goinge to Judda, offringe to bringe aboarde our shipps,
            what packes wee would to be opened there, and to carrie back what wee
            refused/

May   5   I agreed with Sir Henry, to trade for Callicoes with the Junckes, for
            my one thirde parte, which formerlie Sr Henry would in nowise harken
            vnto, but nowe was content to accept of the two third parts for himselfe.

       7   The Thomas and the Darling arived from the Bab/

       9   I caused the Indian shippes to be measured by my Carpenter, which were
            founde to be of the scantlinges followinge / viz /

	Foote
The Rehemee was long from stemm to sternepost	153
Her Rake from the Post afte	017
From the topp of her side in breadth	042
Her debth	031
The Mahomedee in length	136
Her Rake Afte	020
In breadth	041
In depth	029 ½
Her mayne mast in length was 36 yardes	108
Her mayne yarde 44 yardes	132

            The other were not much lesse/

      10   Captayne Mamee came from Moha, to treate with Sr Henrye,
            concerninge his demaundes, But first hee came aboarde the Cloave,
            where hee was frindelie entertained, and after I went with him aboarde
            the trade, where hee delivered to Sr Henrie two letters one from the Basha
            of Sinan, and the other for the Aga of Moha. The effect was to knowe
            what hee demaunded of them, for they were ignorant of anie after wee
            miurie offred to him, And for the former, they said, that they had given
            him satisfaction before his departure/ Wherefore they intreated that the
            Junckes might be discharged and sent for Moha/ His aunswer was
            that hee demaunded satisfaction for the losse of his menns lives, And for
            the makinge of him lose his Monson, to the overthrowe of his voiage/
            Mamee said, if hee would write his minde hee should have aunswer from
            the Basha in 14 daies/

                                                            Captaine/

1612   Assab road

May — 12   Captaine Mamee returned with letters from Sr Henrie.
           The effect as Mamee said was, That the Basha should quit him
           one hundred thowsand Royalls of 8 and to bringe the Junckes to
           Moha /

The king of Rehita
ridinge vppon a Cowe
           15 The kinge of Rehita, being a pettie prince vppon the Affriçan or
               Abeshside came ridinge downe vppon a Cowe to visitt Sr Henrie
               and my self. He had a Turbant on his heade, a peece of a Periwinckle=
               shell hanginge on his forehead insteede of a Iewell. Apparelled like a
               Moore all naked savinge a Pintado about his loynes, attended with
               150 men in Bataile after theire manner, weaponed with Dartes,
               Bowes and arrowes and Swordes and Targettes / Wee went on
               shoare with 100 shott and Pike to prevent all treacherie, that the
               Turkes might plott against vs, by culor of his curtesie, being loath
               to lett him returne without an Enteruiewe, least wee should
               want the refreshinge which wee might haue by his frindshipp heere
               at Asab, which is vnder his commaunde. Wee presented him with
               divers giustes and according to his desire, did giue him his ladinge of
               Aqua vitæ, that he was scarce able to stande. They are Mahometans
               and a black hard favoured people, with Curle pates. The kinge
               bestowed vppon vs five Bullocks and proffered all the assistance he
               might doe vs. This daie the Peppercorne arived from Aden
               bringinge with her a Juncke which came from Sinde or the River
               Indus, laden with Butter, Oile and Cambaia Cloth. They brought
               vs newes, that Mallacamber Captaine of the greate Shipp of
               Diu, had escaped them with his Shipp, and was arived at Moha
               passinge in sight of them. The Peppercorne shott at her, but
               could not reach her, shee went soe well. This was the shipp for
               which the Peppercorne had purposelie waited, and which the Thomas
               and Darlinge had soe longe expected, to haue come to Babo /

           This daie I had a note deliuered me of the prices of comodities howe
           they were latelie bought and soulde at Surat, whereof the coppie
           followeth /   viz t

           Broadcloth of xxmt the cloth severall cullers 20 Mamoodis /
           The Couido of 35 inches, and 5 Mamoodies make one Royall of 8 /
           Reshes. 84 Mamoodies the peece which was lesse then ours did cost
           in England /
           Leade the greate Maunde 33 pounde at 7¾ Mamodyas /
           Tynne the small Maunde 25 pounde at 5½ Royalls of 8 / at
           Dabull /
           Iron the Bahar conteyninge 360 pounde at 21 Rialls of 8 the
           Bahar /
                                                        Peeces —

1612   The Red sea

May 15 Peeces Damasked from 12 to 18 Royalls the peece/
         Elephantes teeth 65 Mamoodeis the greate Maunde of 33 pounde/
         Indico Cirkesa three sortes, whereof the best at 14 Rupias, which make ½
         a R: of 8. The second sorte 12 Rupias, The thirde sorte 8. the greate
         Maunde of 33 pounde/
         Indico Lahor which is best of all 3 sortes, whereof the best at 36. the second
         at 30. the thirde at 24 Rupias, the maunde of 55 pounde/
         Charges of bringinge it to the waterside 10 p cent for Cirkesa And 20
         p cent custome for Lahor/

     17 Wee begann to waighe leade and deliver our English comodities to the
         Captaines masters of the Iunckes, in parte of payment of the goodes wch
         wee had receaued of them

*The Thomas is
dispatched for   23 The Thomas, manned with 49 menn, all in health, sett saile for Zocotora
Zocotora –   for Aloes, And from thence to Priaman and Teco vppon Sumatra
Priaman & Teco.*   for Pepper

     31 The messenger from the Basha of Sinan, the Sabander of the Bannians
         at Moha and Captaine Mamee arriued at Assab, to compounde the
         Differences with Sir Henry Midleton/

June 24 The Trade sett saile out of Assab roade for Moha and the 25. daie the
         Cloaue did followe. The same night they in Moha made greate Bonfiers
         and Fierworkes which for that they had not donne the like before when
         wee were there wee supposed them therewith to braue vs, I sent my Skiff
         to the shoare with letters to the Aga the Sabander and Captaine Mamee
         and gaue the Cokson charge not to put ashoare for feare of surprisinge/
         The effect of these letters was to see what ready monies might be procured
         to cleere the Accompts betwixt the Indians and vs/

     29 The Governour returned an aunswer more ceremonious then of substance
         So that the 30 daie wee returned againe to Assab roade/

Iulie 1 The Trade came thither likewise, and fell to our ould trade of Bartring
         for Indian comodities/

     5   Mere Mahumood Tookee Captaine of the Rehemi of Surat (which
         was the Queenes mothers shipp) brought diuers dishes of meate aboarde
         the Cloaue being dressed after there fashion, hee was accompanied with
         diuers of his principall marchauntes whoe were all kindelie entertained/
         His shipp was at the least of 1200 tunne/

     11 Wee all viz: The Cloaue, Hector, Trade, and Peppercorne, waighed Anker
         to sett saile for Moha together with 7 of the Indian shipps went, which for
         the most parte of them were better then anie of vs any way, In the eveninge
         wee Ankored short of Moha/

     12 Wee waighed and stood for Moha and about 3 in the afternoone wee all anko-
         red before the Towne of Moha/

1612   Moha.

Iulie   18   One of the Junckes which was indebted to vs gott in so neere the shoare
             that wee doubted shee would steale all her goods ashoare. Whereuppon ye
             next daie the Cloave and the Peppercorne did warpe neerer, and discovered
             many Jelbaes aboarde the Juncke to vnlade her, but at their goinge a
             shoare, the Cloave Hector and Peppercorne made many shott at them, soe
             as the menn forsooke both the Junckes and the Jelbaes and swome ashore
             The Castell, nor Towne, not once shootinge at vs, albeit wee were much
             with in commaunde of theire Ordinaunce /

        20   The Gallies fearinge our cominge soe neere, warpt behinde an Islande
             to the Northward /

August   7   Wee had advice of the arrivall of the greate shipp of Sues and 4 greate
             Gallies at Bogo, a Towne on the Abess side about halfe a daies saile from
             Moha /

             I receaved a letter from the Governour of Moha, shewing that this day
             was festivall amongest them and that thereon they were accustomed to
             shoote of sixten peeces of Ordinaunce, desiringe that it might not be taken
             in evill parte, doubtinge leaste wee should hould it donne in a bravado
             and soe, in requitall shott, into the Towne againe /. About noone they
             discharged 17 peeces of Ordinaunce out of the forte, 3 from the landing
             place and divers within the land with aboundance of smale shott, wch
             went of, in good order, some of theire greate shott went a heade of vs,
             and some a sterne, to shewe what they coulde doe, but all past in kindenes
             hereby wee founde the reporte of this place false, vizt that there were
             onelie two peeces and that they were not able in two howers to
             discharge them /

The Hector depar-   8   The Hector sett saile for Priaman and Tecoo (the Monson nowe servinge)
teth for Priaman   havinge 88 English in perfect health /
and Tecoo /

             The Kohodias or Captaines of the Junckes desired to haue Passportes
             from me, for theire better gettinge into theire countrie in case they should
             meete with anie more of our nation, which was graunted /

        10   All reckoninges were cleered with the three Junckes, the Hasani, Caderi,
             and Mahomodi /

        11   wee cleered the Rehemi and Salameti /

             Nota our whole cargason of Commodities and Royalles bartred for
             in this place did amount but to 46174 Royalls of 8

English comodities   At this porte of Moha wee founde not our English comodities vendible
not vendible in anie   for anie quantitie, The naturalls poore, and the Turkes vnwillinge to
quantitie at Moha /   deale with vs /

Wee departed for   13   Wee sett saile from Moha for Bantam, our Companie 75 men all in
Bantam in Iana /   perfect health /

        14   In the morninge in sight of Babo, but the winde large at N.W. wee steered
             E by S through the greate channell on the Abess side, havinge 18 fathom
             about one league of the Islande Babo, where is verie good and safe harbor
                                                                                    for

1612.   From Zacotora to Sumatra

August 14   for shipping and of good receipt, but the place is barren.

September 3   Wee arived at Zacotora in the roade Delisha, having byn much hindred in our passage thether, by a W and N.W. current.

Wee vnderstood that the Thomas had bene heere 3 monethes past, but stayed not, for that they could not agree vppon the price of Aloes.

4   The marchant and Linguist went sent ashoare, and there were kindelie entertayned and furnished with horses to returne to the Skiffe, but could not agree vppon the price, hee houlding it at 40 Royalls of 8 the kintall of 104 pound, saying hee had onelie 25 C. weight, for which hee was earnestlie solicited by the Portingales.

Being loath to loose time heere it was concluded that hee should haue 30 R. for one parcell and 38 for another, soe hee delivered 4067 lb which cost 1418 ½ R. of 8. Wee founde the King verie false both in his waight and worde, but wee vsed him kindelie for the good of future voyages.

8   Wee sett saile for Bantam.

22   Lattitude by the starr 8d. 12. minutes the winde at W.S.W. wee steered E and by S. About midnight wee fell into the strangest and fearefullest shyninge water, that ever came of, vs had seene, the water giveing such a glare about the shipp as that wee could discerne a letter in the booke thereby, it being not halfe an hower before soe darke, as that it was not possible to see half our shipps length anie waie. Wee doubted it had byn the breach of sunken grounde, and thought to haue caste about, but finding that wee had sailed in it for half an hower, and sawe noe alteracio wee held on our course quartering verie much winde and at length, it prooved to be Cuttell fish which made this fearfull shewe.

Cuttell fish yelding a woonderfull glare in the night.

27   In the morning wee had sight of the Jsland Selon, bearing N.E. and by E. about 7 leagues of, being verie high land vpp into the countrie but lowe to seaward.

29   About noone wee fell with Cape Comorin, bearing E. and by S. about 14 leagues of, being highe land, and towardes the north shewing doble land, Neere the waterside, wee sounded and had noe grownde at 100 fathom.

Cape Comorin 7 d. 42. minute.

Note that this lieth in the latitude of 7. 42 m. to the northward of the Lyne, But in our Platts it is made to stand in 6 d. 10 m. which differs one degree 32 minutes, stretching S.S.E. By experience wee finde that it lieth more northerlie, and in our course wee had not sight of anie of the Jslandes co discribed in our Platts, Neither did wee discover anie of the Maldiva Islands whereof the number is said to be soe greate, making our attempt to haue passed betweene the maine and the northerne coast of the Maldives, in 8 d. 00. m. Discrying noe land, vntill wee sawe this mayne.

false Platte

October 15   Lat 4 d. 49 m. to the S.ward of the Lyne. This daie wee had sight of Sumatra whereof the E. most part did beare E.N.E. 14 leagues of high land, heere wee founde a verie stronge current settinge to the S.ward, which put vs of from the land.

Lat 4 d. 49 m. Sumatra

1612. Bantam in Iaua maior.

October

15 Nota, That those bounde for the Straightes of Sunda, must keepe Sumatra aboarde after they are come into old 30m. Siward of the lyne, for there begynneth the current / keepe 30 leagues off with good lookinge out, for there are manie Cayos 15 or 20 leagues of, which by reason of the current wee did not see /

18 Lat. 5d. 20m. way. E. Northerly, verie tempestuous thunder and lightenninge, verie fearefull with much rayne, so that wee could not see the land, But praised be god, notwithstandinge the evill weather, our people were then all in as good health (if not better) as when wee ptéd out of England,

24 Wee came to an Anker in the roade of Bantam, where (though contrarie to expectation) wee founde the Hector which arived there the daie before with the James, in her companie, and certen Flemmynges / The Arivall of all these shipps, and dailie expectaton of the Trades increase the Peppercorne, Darling and Thomas to followe, occasioned a greate though sudden alteration in the prices of comodities. Those of our request being raised verie neere to thrice the value of what they were bought for the daie before the Hectors arivall / Cloves which the marriners of the Hector and James, had bought the daie before for 16 R̃s of 8 the Peecull were nowe risen to 40 R̃s and vpwardes / Pepper the daie before was at 10 R̃s of 8 the 10 sackes, but vppon our cominge was raised to 12 and ½ R̃s, &c /

Wee arived in the road of Bantam the James /

26 I went on shoare and soe to the Courte accompanied with the merchaunts and gaue diuers Presents to the Gouernour Pangran Chamarra, who is as Protector to the kinge ruling all, The kinge being as (noe bodie, though of yeares sufficient) which Presents hee well accepted / wee desired his Order, for speedie landinge of our goods, which hee graunted / Provided that the kinges officers might be acquainted with what wee landed, that the kinge might not be wronged in his Custome /

28 I receaued a letter from William Adams out of Japan, which was redd to all the merchaunts, that they might take notice of the hopes of that Countrie /

A letter of willm Adams from Japan /

Itt was nowe concluded vppon, that, in regarde the Flemminges were soe stronge and allmost sole commaunders of the Moluccas and Banda and y[e] this place heere, is soe vnhealthfull besides our people dangerouslie disorderinge themselues with drinck and women ashoare, the Hector should with all speede be dispatched for England and that 14000 sarkes of Pepper should be provided, for the ladinge of her and the Thomas, Doubtinge that if ones there should come newes of the other shippes expected, Pepper would be much raised ouer nowe it was / wee bargained with Larkmey for 2000 sarkes of Pepper at 127 ½ R̃s of 8 the 100 sarkes, And with Reewee for 1000 sarkes at 125 Royalls the 100 sarkes / And for 3000 sarkes more at 150 R̃s the 100. Wee made triall on shoare, what a Peecull of Cloues might waighe by our English waightes and founde it to be 132 lb subtill true waight /

G. L Penry.

1612   Bantam.

November 9   Sir Henrie Midelton arrived at Bantam in the Peppercorne.
         15   The Governour havinge earnestlie requested it, there mustred before the
              Courtt 40 men out of the Cloave and Hector, 30 out of the Peppercorne,
              and 10 out of the Salomon, in all 80 men, which gaue him good content.
              The Flemmges havinge denied him, It was for the breakinge vpp of the
              Mahometans tent.
         17   Agreed with Keewee for 4000 sarkes of pepper at 16 $$ the 10 sarkes w{th}
              allowaunce of 3 p{r} cent basse.
         18   Heere arived 2 saile of Flemmges, greate shipps, and the Thomas in there
              Companie, shee had gotten at Priaman onelie 312 Baharrs of Pepper and
20 Taile of gould 20 Taile of gould.
         22   One hundred Flemmges with there furniture, and otherwise theire Pike
              men in bright Armor, marched to the Courte where they brought them selues
              into a ringe and gaue three vollies of shott. The Governour sent worde to
              them that the kinge thancked them, That they had donne enoughe, and
              might departe with theire Iron hatts, for soe the Iauans call headpeeces.
         28   Three holland shipps laden for the most with pepper and mare sett saile
              homeward bounde, 5 more of theire shipps sett saile for Banda and the
              Moluccas.

December 4   A dutch shipp arived heere from Choromandell by whome wee vnderstood
The Gloabe in Patane   that they left the Gloabe in Patane bounde for Syam.
bound for Syam
         11   The Hector sett saile from Bantam for Morough the wateringe place where
              there is a sweete aier and where good refreshinge of Ornges and other wholesome
              fruites are to be had. There to attende untill the Thomas were full laden.
         22   The Trades increase and the Darling arived heere from Pryaman.
         25   In honnor of the Birthday of our Saviour Christt texten Chambers were
              discharged at the English howse in Bantam, and were answered with
              ordinaunce out of the shipps.
Keewee a theef   28 Keewee the cheef China Marchant invited Shenrie and my self, with all the
China Marchants   Marchauntes to dynner, and caused a plaie to be acted before vs by ye
curtesie   Scenicks of China, which was performed on a Stage, with good pronunciaton
                     and gesture.
              The Thomas sett saile for England, having in her 636 english and 3 Indians.

January 12   And the 14 in the morning I waighed out of the roade of Bantam for
Wee departed   Japan, havinge taken in heere for that place 700 sarkes Pepper, for a triall
for Japan from   there. I had 74 English, one Spaniard, one Japan and 5 Swarts or
Bantam   Indians.
         15   In the morninge little winde at West and halmg in to 14 fathom, steered
              E and by S. and E.S.E. leavinge Pulo Lacke on our Starboard and
              11 or 12 Islands on her Larboard side. Our depth from 14 to 10 fathomes,
              goinge within two Islandes which lye to the Eward of Pulo Lacke and
              in the fairwaie there lieth a Shoale which hath not about 6 foote on the
              topp of it, and is not about half a Cables length overie waie, and hard aboard
                                                                                    it.

1612   Iaccatra

Ianuarie   15

it, there is 10 fathoms and the next cast on ground, As by experience for heere wee laie three howers, beatinge with a stiff Gale. But through Gods mercie and extraordinarie labours and indeavour of the Company gott her of, but sprunge leake, that for all night and untill ten of the Clock next daie wee contynued pumping everie man (my selfe onelie excepted) taking his turne, and all little enough to keepe it from increasinge which made us all to doubt, that wee should be inforced to put back againe to Bantam, to the overthrowe of our men and voiage for Japan. The Carpenter by his diligence having found out the Leake made it tight (thanked be to God) Nota. That to goe cleere of this shoall, keepe close to the Islandes, for the mayne is shoall.

Wee came on grounde

16   Wee Anchored at the watring place called Tinga Jaua being 14 Leagues from Bantam, and some 3 and a halfe leagues to the westward of Jaccatra, riding betweene two Islandes, which lye of the point, distant 5 miles, depth 10 and 9 fathoms, close to the Islandes.

Tinga Java 2 Islandes

I sent Presents to the king, his Sabandar, and Admirall requesting leave to buie such comodities or necessaries as wee wanted.

18   The king of Jaccatra sent his cheefman unto me with thankes for the Presents, and profer of what his countrie afforded.

21   Wee sett saile and steered next unto the Estermost Islande of the two that are against the watringe place, depth 10 and 9 fathom, and soe to seaboarde of all the Islandes E.N.E. from the watringe place, for the outermost of them beareth E and by N Northerlie. And of the Northerne pointe of the said Island lyeth a shoale, which you shall see breake, distant from the Island halfe a league. And having that S:oof you, the Estermost pointe of Jaua will beare E.S.ly. depth 17 and 18 fathom. And all the waie out from 20 to 14 fathom. But heere you shall finde a current settinge E.S.E. which you must allowe for, as you have the winde. In the eveninge wee ankred, little winde at N by W, the current settinge us to the S.E. uppon the shoare depth 13 and 13½ fathom, being shott 3 leagues to the Ewards of the E.pointe of Jaccatra. winde at N.W.

a Current

22   The winde at S.W wee waighed and steered E.N.E. to gett deepe water and findinge 14 fathom, the highe hill over Bantam did beare W.S.W.½ pointe W.ly. The outward pointe that is to the Ewards of Jaccatra S.W by S. 3½ leagues of, and another pointe to the E.warde bearinge S.E by E. with a greate round hill over it, upp in the land that was the outwardmost land wee did see, steering E.N.E and at noone had 16 and 17 fathom: esteeming the shipp to be some 10 Leagues from the E.land of Jaccatra, and at 4 afternoone wee had 23 fathom and steered E by S. and all night E by S. and E by S. and E.S.E. and had 23 and 24 fathoms.

23   Morninge wee dorst upp our sailes, the winde at S.E. and had sight of an Island which lieth of Cherribon with three of those piked hills of Java, the E. most bearinge S.E. and Cherybon S by E. Latitude at noone 6d. 10.m.

the winde

1612   Pulo Labuc

Ianuarie 23 The winde at N N W, the Island bearing E by N 3½ leagues off wee
              sounde with our skiffe, rounde about the Islandes 23 and 24 fathomes,
A ledge of   within sacker shott of the shoare and then noe grounde at 30. And off the N
Rockes aboue   pointe there lieth a ledge of rockes aboue water, and on the S end, a lowe
water   spott with a tree or two vppon it, hauing made an E by S way, 15 leagues
              since yesterdaie at noone and in Longitude from Bantam 44 leagues
              Nota That yo[u] maie bouldlie keepe betweene 23 and 24 fathom water
              in the offing, and in 20 fathom vppon Iaua, the darkest night that is,
              and in the daie vppon Iaua in what depth you please, There are many
              deepe bayes and highe hills in the Countrie, but the land to the seaside is
              verie lowe at 6 at night the Island did beare N W by W about 10 leagues
              off wee steered E S E and E by S all night depth 25 and 26 fathom,
              the winde at W N W.

          24 In the morninge wee had sight of three high piked hills and three other
              to the E ward like Islandes depth 20 fathom, the pointe of Iaua bearing
              S E and by S And the Island lying off it S E and N W about 9 leagues
              off wee steered E and by S and E ¾ E Latitude 6 degrees 10 m. Way E
              28 leagues, ffrom noone wee steered E and by S wind at N N W.
              depth, 27 fathom And at 2 of the clock the wind came to the W N W
              and blewe hard Wee continued our course E and by S and at midnight
              had 26 fathom At two in the morninge at 22 fathom and the neerer
              the shoare, we founde the harder grownde, and to the offinge oaz Then
              wee stood off N E and N N E till daie, and the lowe land to the W ward
              of the N pointe of the land S S W and the sadd old lowe land S E and
              by S 4 or 5 leagues off And an Island off it N W and by N about foure
              leagues Then wee steered E N E but the best course from the Island
Cobina a head= aforesaid is to steere E and by S for that will bringe you in the middest
Land   betweene the headland, which is called Cóbina and the Island which
              lieth off it S Wly 5 leagues, It is a headland with a smale Island off y
              S E pointe, And if it be cleere you shall see three sharpp highe hills over
              the lowe pointe one equallie distant from thother, and are called the three
              Hermanos Alsoe you shall see highe land to the E ward rise like an
              Island, but come not neerer then 20 fathom in the nighte Latitude at
              noone 6 degrees 16 minutes. Way. E and by S halfe a pointe S'ly 16 leagues
              The smale Island at noone bearinge S W and by W 7 leagues off

          25 Wee steered E the winde at W and by N keepinge in 30 fathom

Poolo Labuck 26. At breake of daie wee had sight of the Island called Poolo Labuck bearing
              N E and by E 8 leagues off winde W and by N Wee steered E and by S
              depth 34 and 35 fathom and about 9 of the clock had sight of land
              bearinge S E and S E and by S The Island aforesaid bearinge now N E
              and by N little winde, Lattitude 6 degrees 12 minutes Way E and by N
              22 Leagues, winde at West The Island at 4 in the afternoone bearinge
              W and by N 9 leagues off, Depth 34 fathom

                                                                    Lattitude

1612   Celebes

Ianuarie 27. Lattitude 6 degrees 4 minutes, way E N ly 28 leagues depth 38 fathom, and at 3 in the afternoone had sight of an Island bearinge N N E 7 leagues off and at 5 of the clock sounded and had 34 fathoms The Island bearinge N and by E about 5 leagues of, winde at N W and by W, wee steered E and by N till 12, then had 24 fathom The w Island N W halfe a pointe W ly, then E depth 24 fathom / Nota That when wee came into 20 fathom wee did finde hard grounde but in the faire waie Oaz, and the Island N off vs, our depth did dicrease to 17 and 18 fathom and soe continewinge betweene it and 24 vntill the Island did beare N W and by W and then 24 fathom, And steeringe from the first shoald, E kepe in this depth.

28. At 4 in the morninge wee had 25 fathom steeringe E till noone Latt 5 degrees 55 m. Wa E N ly 20 leagues depth 30 fathom, ffrom noone wee steered E by S and at 4 a clock had 35 fathom.

29. In the morninge about 4 winde at W by N wee steered E by S but had noe grounde at 40 fathom, but at noone 52 fathom with many w w overfalls Lattitude 6 d. 09 m. Way E by S 28 leagues winde at W and W by N with a current settinge to the W warde Afternoone wee sounded but had not grounde at 100 fathom and steered E.

30. In the morninge Lattitude 5 d. 57 m. Way E N ly 28 leagues and in longitude from Bantam 224 leagues the over falls continewinge but soundinge had not grounde at 100 fathom. At 3 in the afternoone wee had sight of a lowe flatt Island at topmast heade bearinge N E by N 5 or 6 leagues off, full of trees and had 18 fathom, and at nexte past 85 fathom Then wee steered E by S and at 4 a clock it did beare N by E ½ p. N ly 3 or 4 leagues off Then wee had sight of two other lowe flatt Islandes, the one openinge to the E ward the other to the W ward soe that this was the middelmost At 6 at night, it bearinge N ½ p. E ly Wee sounded againe but had not grounde at 80 fathom, wee steered E by S keepinge our leade in respect of the over falls or riplinge which wee was fearefull, yet had noe grounde at 60 fathom.

Celebes   31. At breake of daie wee had sight of the Celebes the wester end risinge like an Island and the outtermost highe land, bearinge E by N Latitude 5 d. 52 minutes, the E part bearinge E by N 6 leagues off way E N ly 16 leagues and a current settinge to the Northwestward.

Wee had sight of a Iuncke which wee stood with depth 24 fathom 2 or 3 leagues of the lowe land that is vnder the highe land, wee edged into 12 ffathom to speake with her, The Pynnas was sent forth and brought the maister aboard, of whome wee informed our selues for our better passage throughe the Straightes, This Iunck was bound for Amboyno, and belonged to a greater Iunck of the ~ fleminges which wee discried aheade some 3 leagues of. At Sunn settinge wee tooke in our sailes to keepe short of the Straightes of Desalon

The straight of Desalon or Solore   by the naturalles called Solore, and keepinge our leade all night wee sounded.

1612 The Straight of Desalon

Ianuarie 31 founde; first 20 fathom, the highe sand N: and soe drove into 33. and 47 fathum, fearinge a shoald, which lieth two mile from the Celebes, and at lowe water the breath vppon it maie be seene. On the Celebes side it is verie dangerous and full of suncken grounde wherefore wee hal'd over for Desalon side, keepinge a good birth of it, having a piked hill which is next to the seaside risinge like an Island beinge to the W: wardes, then it is N.N.E. and when it is N: then you are thwart of the west end of the shoald and then will the Island which yu leave on your starr board side, beare E.N.E. soe that you maie be boulde to steere out in the middest betweene the two Islandes. And when the piked hill beares N and by W: then art you thwart of the E: end. Nota That the E: end of Desalon sheweth like an Island, and will deceave you till you come to it but havinge brought the N: ende of the pointe E.N.E halfe a pointe Easterlie, then be boulde, for you are cleare of the shoald aforesaid. It is about 4 leagues betweene them. Wee came within halfe a mile of the Islande leavinge it on our starrboard side goinge through, and the winde takinge vs sudden lie short, wee sonded, but had noe grounde at 55 fathom right vpp and downe.

February 1 Afternoone wee were thwart of the pointe of the Islande bearing S. of vs, and the two Islandes which make the Straightes, lyinge one from the other N and S: distant 5 smale leagues, from hence wee steered E: and by N, the winde at N and N. and by E: accomptinge the distance betweene Bantam and this place of the straights 265 leagues. Wee had sight of a greate Iunck of Pattany bound from Boyno. J sent my Pinnasse to knowe what shee was and they brought 3 flemings with them which were passengers in her, theire owne shipp beinge wrackt vppon the Island called Burneo not farr from Soocadana.

An Hollan. ship cast away vpon the Isle of Burneo.

2 In the morninge, wee had sight of the south parte of Desalon S.W and by S. and the N: parte W and by N. 8 leagues of. wee steered. E. and by N. the winde at N and by E: Latitude 5 degrees 52 minutes. Distant from Desalon 10 leagues. About 3 afternoone wee had sight of Cambina bearing N.E. the north parte risinge like a Humock or Island, bearing N.E. ½ point Northerlie 12 leagues of.

Cambina

3 In the morninge the southern ende of Cambina did beare N.E. and by E: and the Island or Humork N.E. 8 leagues of. Latitude 5d. 57m. The Island N.E. halfe a pointe northerlie 8 leagues way. E.S.E. 6. leagues, winde at S: wee steered, E. and by N.

4 In the morninge the winde at N.E. Latitude 5 degrees, and at 3 in the afternoone, wee had sight of land bearinge E and by N: making it to be the Island Bootun.

5 Fower leagues of Cambina, wee founde the current to runne vs to the Northward the winde at E: and by N.

6 At breake of day the Island N.E. and by N: 4 leagues of the winde at N: soe that these 24. howers, wee were gotten to the E: wardes one pointe

1612.   The Island of Botun.

February   7   Breake of daie, the Northern pointe was N. and by E: and a
                        small high land that lieth to the S: warde 6 or 7 leagues of Bootun
                        S.E. and the Easterland of Bootun E.N.E, wee steered E and by N.
                        and E. but left the high land to the S: wardes on our Starrboard side,
                        and it did beare S.E.&Ely, Then was the pointe of Bootun shutt in, in
                        alonge greatt Island, the Northerend will be N.N.W. This Island and
                        the other lieth N.N.W. and S.S.E, the winde at N.W; wee steered
                        with the E. pointe and betweene the E. parte of Cambina and the
                        Westerparte of Bootun, is 8 or 9 leagues Lattitude, 5 degrees 54 m.

The Island of   8   In the morninge wee sawe another Island called Tingabasse, risinge
Tingabasse   rounde and flatt, heere wee had a current setting N.E. the winde at
                        N.E. and by N:

                    9   Winde at N.W. and by N: the pointe of Bootun. N.W. wee had sight of
Mr Welden an   two Curra Curraes, betweene it and Bootun: I sent my skyffe of
Englishman   to them, and they broughte one Mr Welden one of the Expeditions
imploied in the   companie and a Fleminge bounde for Banda aboarde, the said Welden
King of Bootunes   beinge imploied in the kinge of Bootunes affaires, for Banda and had
service   nowe the commaunde of these Curra Curraes, Latitude 5d 20 m.
                        Winde at E.N.E. wee steered N. and at nyght the winde S'ly, wee
                        steered N.N.E. and from the Easternmost pointe of Bootun, the land
                        falleth awaie sodenlie, with two or 3 greate Bayes to the N.W. warde
                        and 3 greate Islandes, which lye to the N: ward of Bootune which
Aduertisemts   maketh the Straightes / Nota. To goe throughe the straightes of
concerning the   Bootune it is not about a league broade, and the entraunte is on
straightes of   the N: side of the Island. And if you come from the W: warde beinge
Bootun   thwarte of the N.W. pointe, your course is. E.N.E. and E and by N.
                        and no danger but what you shall see, But you must leave the 3
                        greatt Islands to the N: wardes of you: but goe not betweene
                        anie of them, And fallinge with the Westerend of Bootun, goe not
                        betwene the Island, that lieth of it for there are two longe Islandes
                        but leave them on your starboardside, for it is full of broken groimd
                        betweene them and Bootun / But if the winde serve you, then
                        goe to the N: warde of all the Islandes, either betweene Bootun,
                        and Cambina or els to the N. warde of that too / And soe you
                        maie keepe the coast of Celebes, for it is boulde /

                   10   In the morninge the straughtes of Bootun did beare N.W. and
                        by W. and the maine Island of Tingabese. S.S.E. and at
                        noone, the N. Island, N.W. and by N. 7 leagues of haumge
                        made a N.N.E. way from 4 yesterdaie in the afternoone 13
                        leagues, The winde at S.S.W. /

1612   The Island Machian.

Februarie 11 At 5 in the morninge the winde at N.W. the Island W. 10 leagues of. wee steered N.N.E. Latitude at noone 4d. 8 minutes. way N.N.E. Ely a little. 24 leagues and of the E. pointe of Bootiu 35 leagues, the winde all night between N. and N. by W.

12 The winde at N. and by W. Lat: 4d. 6 minutes. way. E. and by N. 20. leagues

13 In the morninge wee had sight of the Islande Burro, beinge high land the one pointe bearinge E. and by N. and thother E.N.E. 10 leagues of. The winde at N. and by W. wayes 7 leagues Latitude 3 degrees, 41 minutes.

14 In the morninge wee bore vpp with the E. parte of the Island to seeke for some place to ride in, but founde it so deepe shore to, that wee could not come to Anker.

16 Breake of day the Northermost parte of Burro did beare E. and by N. 9 leagues of. Lattitude, 3 d. 40. m. winde at. E.N.E.

17 Little winde, the E. parte of Burro bearinge E. Norterly winde at N. and the Northermost parte of the same Islande, E. and by S. wee had sight of 3 Islandes bearing N. E. and by N.

18 In the morninge wee were by the Easternmost Island 3 leagues of, winde at N.N.W. yt bearing N.N.E. Att noone wee were within a mile of the shoare, I sent of the Skiff to speake with the Cuntrie people, by whome wee vnderstoode that this Islande was called *Sula*. wee had 15 fathom the shippes length of the shoare, and a mile of not grounde at 100 fathum. The west parte of Burro lying S. 2 pointes W. ly. and N. ½ a pointe easterlie. 14 leagues thence from thother, winde at W. and the land stretchinge N.N.E. beinge alonge Island, wee steered away N.N.E.

The Island of Sula

20 Winde at E. and by N. wee steered N. and by E. Latitude 1 degree 30 minutes. way N.E. 7 leagues The northermost land wee did see bearinge N.

21 Wee were 4 or 5 leagues of an Islande called Haleboling by our Sailers, beinge a high topped winde Island different in shappe from all the rest of the Islandes in sight, the winde at N.E. and at E. havinge made to this noone a North. E. waye 4 leagues Latitude 1 degree 16 minutes. The pointe of Haleboling or Bachan N.E. and by N. 4 leagues of. And the outtermost lande N. a quarter W. ly, findinge a current settinge N.E.

The Isle Bachian by the English Sailers called Haleboling.

22 In the morning wee had sight of land N. and by E. It beinge the Island Mackian, verie high land. heere wee had a current setting N.N.E. latitude at noone 0 d. 51 minutes. variation at
                                                                             Sunne

1612   Bachiah

February 22 Sunne setting 04d 12 minutes, windeat N by E. and N. N. E.

23 In the morning wee were 3 leagues of the land, winde at N. N. E. seeking a place to anker in, and within a quarter of a mile of the shoare had 40 fathom, whereof wee bore vpp to the S.ward parte of the Island where wee had 20 and 19 fathom: for a cast or 2 but then noe grounde wee steered from this S. pointe E.S.E. for soe the land lieth open of the pointe of the hyght round Island, being 4 leagues betweene the two pointes. But the wester pointe is an Island with 3 or 4 other to the Eward, which you cannot perceave, till you be verie neere them. Then the land falleth away N. E. and sheweth a large rounde sounde or bay, with land of both sides, verie deepe, this rounde hill is Bachian, and yeildeth greate store of cloaves, but by reason of the warres they are wasted. The people not suffered to make theire benefitt thereof, forbeare to gather them and lett them fall and rott vppon the grounde. Beinge by the Flemmings and Spaniardes opprest, and wrought to spoile one another in civill warres, whilest they both standes in stronge fortes, sitt and looke on prepared to take the bone from him that can wrest it from his fellowe. Having noe ground to anker in, and not able to gett to the N.ward wee resolved to stand of all night, hopinge to haue a shifte of winde to carrie vs to the Island Mackian, whether wee intended.

24 In the morninge the highe land S. by E. 10 or 12 leagues of, the Island seemed ragged, wee stoode in, and a league of the pointe, sent of the skiff to sounde, and to looke for water, but returned aboarde findinge noe water, nor place to anker in. Wherefore wee stoode in to the bay, and presentlie had sight of a forte and towne called Bachian, The Pynnasse a heade findinge fresh water in divers places, but steep too into the Codd of the Baye, where the Flemmings haue a forte artificiallie and warlike built, the towne hard by it, Heere wee came to an Anker, (saker shott of the forte) having had verie vncertaine shoalinge, 70. 60. 8 and 10 fathom, but oaze.

The dutch saluted vs with 5 peeces, whome I requited with the like number, but the kinges man being then aboarde our shipp wee told him it was donne to the honor of his kinge, who sent mee worde that hee would haue come to visitt mee, but that the dutch intreated him to forbeare.

In this forte are 13 peeces. viz. one demy culuering of Brasse, the rest saker and minion, The Flemmings heere resident are more feared of the naturalles then loved, which notwithstanding is cause of theire better benefitt. For the naturalles assoone as wee

---

(margin notes:)

A smale fort of the Hollenders

Boa de Bathian being the Northermost end of the Islandes in our platte called Hale-bolinge.

1612   Bachian.

February 24 wee were arived, could vs, that they durst not bringe vs a Catty of Cloaues, but vppon theire liues/

As wee ridd heere the outwardmost pointe was S:S:W: and the other S:W: distant from vs 4 leagues/ The kinge sent his Admirall and diuers of his nobles aboarde to bidd me welcome, sayinge that they knewe of what nation wee were by our Flagge, vsinge muche cermonious curtesie, wishinge that wee were seated theire in steed of the flemings that they might be cleered of them, theire cuntrie nowe allmost ruined by these warres/

I entertained them frindlie and tould them that o' comminge was to procure trade and to leaue a factorie amongest them if theire kinge soe pleased They aunswered, that it was a thinge by them muche desired, but at present not to be graunted, yet they would acquainte theire kinge therewith/

The smale force of the Hollanders in Bachian

The Captaine of the Dutch forte came aboarde to visitt me, by whome I vnderstoode theire forte to be but of 13. peeces and 30. souldiers, the most of them maried, some to the cowntrie women and some to Dutch women whereof the florte was fitted with. 11. able to withstand the furie of the Spaniard or other nation whatsoeuer, beinge of a verie lustie large breede, and furnished with fewe good qualities/ But it seemed they followed theire Leader, for noe sooner was theire captaine aboarde but the Amazon band followed, complayninge of greate miserie, sittinge downe with our sailers to vitualls at theire first cominge with smale intreatie They had what the shipp affoorded, and they returned ashoare with theire Captaine/

March 3 Wee sounded with the skiff alongest the E:side of the bay, and at the openinge or goinge out neere to a little Island wee founde a place to ancker, in 12. 16. 20. fathom, currall grownde without commaunde of the forte/ Nota there is a shoald to the S: wardes the length of 3. Cables Latitude 00°. 50. minutes/

4 The kinge of Ternata sent me a Present by his Priest/

variation 4° 48 m: Esterly

5 variation at Sunne risinge. 4°. 48. m. Ely. A Moore came aboarde with a Muster of Cloaues offringe to sell some quantitie if wee would goe to Machian/ This moore was sent by a mann of greate acc'ompt of that place whoe at the present was heere whereof it was thought good to staie a daie longer to haue some conference with him his name was Key Malladaia and was brother to the ould kinge of Ternata/

Wee staide

1612 — Machian & Tidore

March

6 Wee staied to speake with this Cavalier whoe came and promised to goe with vs to Machian, and to bringe vs to a place there called Tahannee, and did put aboarde vs two of his cheef menn to be as our Pilates thether, appointinge vs to goe before and staie for him at an Island by the waie, and within two daies hee would be with vs, giuinge vs greate incouragement of good store of Cloaues. Hee tould me, that the Dutch gaue 50 Royalls of 8 the Bahar, but they would cost vs 60 Royalls, which I willingly promised to giue.

Nota — Tahannee is a towne vppon Machian, where the Portugalls heeretofore haue had a forte, but nowe there is none neither for them nor the Fleminges. Heere is the best ridinge of the whole Island, but verie neere the shoare, yet free of all danger.

7 In the morninge wee waighed anker and parted out of the roade called Amasan, and by direction of our newe Pilatts steered m. W. and W. and by N. for the Island Machian, leauinge two Islandes, which ly 4 or 5 miles from the place where wee last ankered on our larboard side, Depth 22, 30, and 40 fathom, 2 Cables length of the Island.

10 Wee had sight of Machian, being a high topped Island, bearing N. Ely, and the Island Tidore openinge like a sugerloafe on the wester side, but not soe high land as Machian, being shutt into the point of the wester side of the outermost Islandes of the 3 that lye in the goinge out, two of them being without the narrowe or straight, and the third maketh the straightes it selfe. yet there are more Islandes on the Easter side, but the current setting to the S. wardes wee ankored in 23 fathom, a mile of the little Island, in the straightes mouth, soe that the distance from the straites of Namorat, to this passage is 5 leagues. And from the roade of Amasan, where the flemish fortres standeth 14 leagues.

The roade of Amasan where the Hollanders Fort standeth:—

11 In the morninge wee waighed, the winde at S.S.E: and the current setting to the N: ward, wee passed the Straightes, the winde veered to the Northwest and by N: wee stood to the E: ward till noone, then we tackt to the W: ward, winde at N.N.W. and had sight of a verie greate Island called Gelolo, being a verie long Island, depth comy out 29 and 34 fathom, and manie Islandes to the E. and E.S. Ewardes, the pointe of old Bachan

Gelolo —

1612 　　　　　　　　The Iland Taualli

March 11 old Bachan lying to the N:ward of the Straightes, some 3 or 4
leagues, leaving 4 Islandes on the Starboardside, That which
Taually Bachar maketh the straightes on that side is called Taually Bachar, and when
you are a little without the small Island which lieth in the straightes,
you shall haue 18 fathom a cast or 2, and then it will deepen and
stand into the N: wardes/. You shall open another Island to the
W:ward called Tamata, with a Rock like a saile a good distance of
the pointe thereof. Wee ankored at an Island bearinge N.W.ly
3 leagues from the straightes in 43 fathom. Where on the Sotherne
A Shold pointe is a shoale having 3 fathom on the skirtes thereof, and is dry
at lowe water. Which Shoale reacheth over to the S. parte of
Bachian. Wee ridd halfe a mile of the shoare, This Island is called
Taually, the winde at N.N.W.

12 Heere wee staied all this daie for Keymalladaia being the place
where hee appointed to come vnto mee, This Island is distant from
Machian 10 leagues; Heere wee had good stoare of wood, but noe
water.

13 Our Coopers prouided themselues of Rottans for water caske, which
maketh excellent hoopes and are heere of all Assizes in greate
aboundaunce, The Shole aforesaid now adrie, did beare W and by
S: halfe a mile of, and another pointe a mile of, N.N.E: the winde
at N.

14 ffor that Keymalladaia came not, his seruantes doubted that the
Alemains seeing vs to adventure through this passage amongest the
Islandes did suspect him and perforce kept him; wherefore I did sett
saile, and plied vpp for Machian. The Northern point of Taualli,
and the Northerne pointe of Latitate, from whense wee sett saile,
bearing one of the other W and by N. and E and by S. distant 6 leagues,
And the Norther end of Taualli and the bodie of Grochi, the greate
Grochi a great Island, lye the one from the other N.W. fower leagues and N.N.W
Island from Grochi, are 4 or 5 small Islandes which couer the mayne of
the greate Island and are distant from it 5 leagues N: wardes. And
there are many Islandes N.E. and by N: called Motere. The sounde
lieth cleere of all the Islandes betweene Bachan and Gelole alias
Batachina S.E. and N.W, and is verie broade, but hath Islandes
on the Starrboarde side as you goe to the N: wardes. The Channell
betweene Bachan, Machian, Tidore, and Ternata, lieth N. and by W.
and S. and by E. and is 6 leagues over in the narrowest parte/

Machian.   15 In the morninge wee passed betweene Batachina and Caia. Latitude
leagues of the at noone 17 minutes to the N: wardes;/ Soe that Machian is not truly
Lyne. placed in the Platt, for that there the Equinoctiall cutts it in y middle
and

1612   The roade of Pelebri

March 15. and wee finde it to stand 5 leagues more N^{ly}, winde at N by E
and N by W, with a current settinge to the S wardes. Variation
4 degrees 58 minutes E^{ly}

Caia an Island 16. In the morninge wee went faier by the Island of Caia, winde at N
and by E. Heere wee had sight of a saile standing to the N wardes
which by a ffisherman wee vnderstoode to be a ffleminge, bounde
from Machian to Tidore with Sago, which is a roote, whereof the
naturalles make theire Breade.

A fort of the fleminges called Tabolola 17. In the morninge wee were neere a fforte of the fleminges called
Tabolola, winde at N E. wee stoode to the S wardes, the current setting
vs to the N wardes. Then the winde at E by N. wee steered with the
Estmost pointe, and came to an Ancker at 4 in the afternoone in the
roade of Pelebere, hard by Tahannee in 50 fathom withm call of the
shoare, having one pointe of the sande, S S W. 2 miles off. And another
N E by N. 1½ miles off, and the Island Caia 5 leagues off. This
night some smale quantitie of Cloaues were brought aboard, the
price sett at 60 Royalls of 8 the Bahar of 200 Catties each Cattie
3 pounde 5 ounces English. I receaued a letter from Keymala-
dia from Bachian, expruising his stait, with promise that shortlie hee
would be with me. In the meane time, that hee had written to
the people to help me to all the Cloaues they coulde.

18. A Saniaca came aboard and proffered much curtesie, and two
Hollanders came with him, being verie desirous to knowe whoe
directed vs to this roade, sayinge, that it must needes be one of y^e
Naturalles and that if they knewe him, they would cutt him in
The Hollenders entertaiment of vs peeces before our faces, and that I did wronge them in comminge
hether, this beinge theire countrie, as hauinge conquered it by the
Sworde. I sent worde vnto them, that they should returne to theire
fortes and tell theire Captaines that if they needed aught that I
might spare, they should haue it, for reasonable content before the
Naturalles, because I acknowledged them our heighbours, and
Bretheren in Christe. But for anie propertie of this Countrie
to be more in them then in me, I tooke not notice, and there fore woulde
ride heire, and trade with whosoeuer pleased to come aboarde.
So they parted thrattning the countrie people which went then a
boarde, that iff they did bringe Cloaues vnto me, they would putt
them to death. But they made light of theire threates, and saide
they held the English theire frindes, and would come aboarde me.
Soe that this daie was bought 300 Catties of Cloaues for 2 or 3
Cambaia cloth and some Royalls.

19. The two fleminges came aboarde againe, and begann to note downe
in theire Table bookes the names of the cuntrie people which came

                                             aboarde

1612 — The roade of Pelebri

March 19. aboard, whereuppon I caused the Boateswaine to turne them out of the shipp and commaunded them to come noe more aboarde, and sent divers of my companie on shoare to see what entertainement the Cormbrie people woulde giue them, They went upp to theire townes of Tahannee and Pelebre and were verie kindelie vsed, and tould that the flemings had wrought soe with Key Chillisadang, the Kinge of Tarnataes sonne, whoe was newlie come, that hee had forbidden them to sell vs anie Cloaues vppon paine of death, or otherwise wee should haue had them before the flemings whome they finde greatelie to oppresse them, And towardes Eveninge the Kinge passing by our shipp in his Curra Curra, I sent of my Pinnasse vnto him well fitted viz: with a faier Turkie Carpett, and Crimson silk and gould Curtaines, intreatinge him to come aBoarde, which hee tooke kindelie, but excused it, sayinge That in the morninge hee would visitt me, This daie wee bought 227 Cattees of Cloaues, and sould good quantitie of Cambaia cloth for money

20. This daie was spent in conference and complements with a Saniaca of good accompt, and a Priest that was kinsman to the kinge of Tanata, and the Casis of Tahannee, all three came aboarde, and proffered greate kindenes, Wee traded with the people for 58 Cattees of Cloaues and sould good quantitie of cloth

The spight of the hollanders to vs

21. An Oran Caia came aboarde, and tould me that a Curra Curra of the flemings had taken divers Canoos cominge aboard me with Cloaues threatninge death to them, and that since my cominge hither they had dissurnished all theire forts and placed theire people rounde about ye Island that the naturalls should bringe me not more spice, and that they had sent over a Curra curra to Tidore, to cause two of theire greate shipps to come hether and ride by me, the one ahead the other asterne, and to inforce mee out of the roade without trade or refreshing

22. Wee had sight of one of the flemish shippes cominge about the pointe by reason whereof wee had little trade, the people beinge much afraide, The naturalles expected nowe what would become of vs, the flemings haveing reported on shoare that they should see vs runn out of the roade at sight of one of theire shippes, This day was bought 29 Cattees of Cloaues and sould good stoare of Cambaia Cloth for money

Cambaia cloth very vendable heere

At night the fleminge came and Anckred asterne our shipp within call, the shipp was called the Redd Lyon, haveing 30 peeces of Ordinaunce, The Captaines name Block, whoe came from Holland Generall of 11 saile, Wee did not salute one another, neither by shott nor worde of mouth

23

1612 — The road of Pelebri.

March 23 The Captaine of the flemish shipp attended with manie souldi[ers] went ashoare, and at his landinge had 3 peeces shott out of his shipp, marchinge in state by our shipp, threatninge the naturalls, soe lowde, that wee could heare them aboarde of. I sent three of the Marchantes ashoare well fitted willinge them to walke towardes the fleminges, and findinge them to meete them, to returne the like curtesie, yf not, to take noe notice of them, and passe vpp to the towne, and see what good were to be donne with the naturalls for trade, The flemmiges remayned sitting. Our people accordinge to direction, passed by them to Tahannee and Pelebre, and were well vsed of the naturalles. But the Prince of Ternata had giuen them soe strait a charge, that though they had some Cloaues in theire howses, yet they durst not sell them vnto vs. They tould the Marchauntes, that the fleminges at theire cominge on shoare had protested, that assoone as theire other shipp should arive heere from Tydore which they expected daielie, they would take mee and make prize of the shipp. This daie wee had little or no trade, the people beinge afraide to bringe victualls to vs.

24 The Prince of Ternata Chisillisadang, sent to tell me that hee would come and visitt me, soe all thinges were fitted in good manner for his entertainement. He came attended with diverse greatt Curra currass, and rowed thrise roundt about the shipp before hee entred. At his boardinge, I caused 5 peeces of ordinannce to be shott of, and brought him to my Cabbyn, where I had prepared a Banckett of diverse rare Conserves, and a Consort of Musique which much delighted him. Hee promised mee to giue the people licence to bringe Cloaues aboarde me, and requested that I would but haue patience for a daie or two, that hee might haue advice from his brother then beinge at Tidore, I bestowed on him diverse Presents, and at partinge ordred 7 peeces for his farewell.

25 In the morninge a Curra curra of the flemminges came rowinge by our shipp, scoffinge, and singinge a songe which they had made in derision of vs, The often striue thereof as alsoe theire rowinge over our Can-boies divers times indeavouringe to sinck them, Wherefore I caused the Pynnasse to be well fitted and gaue order, that if at theire returne they continewed theire booyish behaviour, to runn aboarde and sinck them. They came scoffing accordinge to theire accustomed manner, The Pynnasse rann aboarde them with such a shure that the water rann through theire sides, There being in her two of the Captaines of theire fortes well fitted with shott and Dartes, Our men went well provided and had two good Fowlers in the

A Curra curra of the Hollanders almost sunck

1613   The roade of Pelebri.

March. 25 in the skiff head, They laie a good while aboarde her, and willed them to
take this for a warninge, and leave of theire scoffinge and mockinge of vs,
for els they would teach them better manners the next time, and soe
they returned aboarde, with theire promise that it should be soe noe
more. Towardes eveninge they sent one of theire marchaunts vnto
me, with a writinge from theire Doctor in Droits, who (as wee were
informed) was the cheefest amongest them in absence of Butt, The
A writing sent effect whereof was to lett me knowe, That all the people of the
from the Hol- Mollocas had made a perpetuall contract with them, for all theire
landers Cloaues at 50 Royalls of 8 the Bahar of 200 Catties, in respect
that they had delivered them out of the servitute of the Spaniardes,
not without losse of much bloode, and expence of greate wealth,
Willing me that I should not move the people from theire obedience,
which might redounde to theire greate damage, They houldinge the
cuntries to be theire owne as conquered by the sworde. Alsoe that
the naturalles ought them, much money which was advaunced to
be paide in Cloaues

Aunswer was returned, that wee would not meddell with theire
busines our cominge beinge onelie to trade with such as desired to
trade with vs, and soe dismissed him

27. The fleminges inforced the prince to lie with his Curra curra
a sterne to keepe watch, that none bringe anie thinge aboarde vs,
for in our sight he commaunded a Canoa aboarde him which was
cominge to vs (as wee thought with spice) makinge him returne,
Towardes night, two of the naturalles brought vs some refreshinge

28. The prince vnderstandinge that wee tooke it not well that hee ridd
soe neere vs to the feareinge of the naturalles, remooved and went
about a point further of which much discontented the fleminges
Afternoone with the Skiff well manned I went to see, iff I could
deale with the Prince for a parcell of Cloaues, but founde him
gonne to the Westerside. Captaine Block seing my Skyff gonne
in to the Bay, followed vs with his Curra curra, and would have
landed where I was, but that I would not suffer him. Which the
naturalles seinge and that Captaine Block returned aboard againe
without landinge, divers of the better sorte came downe to vs professing
greate love towardes vs, and sent for Cokers and other fruitts and
bestowed them vppon the King. The maister of the Cloaue seeing
Captaine Block to make such speede after vs manned the longe boate
for aide, but vppon a signe given returned aboarde

30 The fleminges brought the prince to ride by vs in his ould place
Towardes eveninge annother flemish shipp came in called the Moone
a propper shipp of 32 peeces of good ordinaunce, but not above 50 men
Shee

1613   Motire.

March.   30 Shee came to an anker soe neere aheade of us, as that wee
              could scarselie winde cleere on of the other / The prince sent
              vnto me to excuse his comming back but nowe wee sawe that
              hee durst not displease the flemings /

          31 Divers harsh dealinges and discurtesies passed betwixt the
              flemings and us /

Aprill   1 The flemings brought 120 of theire menn ashoare which e-
              morninge and eveninge did sett and discharge the watch with
              Drumm, ffyfe and Ensigne. This force they had gathered together
              out of theire fortes and shipped /

           2 I seeinge noe hope of ladinge and that Key Malladria came
              not accordinge to promise, gave order to the maister to cause
              water to be filled, and to make readie to sett saile, with the first
              faier winde /
              At noone, observinge wee found this roade of Pelabry to stand in
              ood. 26. minutes to the N: wardes of the Equinoctiall. Var: 03. 28ᵐ
              the highest land in the Island Machian bearing. W. N. W. ½ point
              Westerly /

           5 Wee wayed anker, little winde, the current settinge to the S: ward
              wee drove to sea, being vnder our foresaile, and aheade the Moone
              the greate shipp of the flemish, which made a faier shott vnder
              our starne, which wee presentlie aunswered close aheade his
              Admirall, expectinge further, but heard not more of them /
              At noone they both wayed and followed vs but the winde at S. W.
              had put vs soe farre to the windewarde, as that the naturalles
              came aboarde with Cloaves for a tyme, as fast as wee could
              weighe and pay for them, the flemings not able to hinder them
              Alsoe there came an Oran Caya aboarde, whoe promised vs
              a good parcell of Cloaves, if wee would but come neerer y shore
              in the morninge /

           6 About 50 Catties of Cloaves were brought aboard in divers
              Canoes, but not riewes of the gallant. Towardes eveninge
              standing neerer the shoare then wee were willinge, but for this
              occasion wee had sight of a West ashoare. The skiffe was sent
              and spake with the Oran Caya whoe said the Cloaves weare
              readie and in the darck should be brought aboarde, but present-
              -ly a Curra curra of the flemings passed by, put him into such
              a feare as albeit our people would haue wafted him yet durst hee
              not adventure, so they returned /

Mootiere   7 In the morninge wee were thwarte of Mootiere being distant
              from the wester pointe of Machian 4 leagues N. by E. ½ point
              Easterlie, And from it N. 3 leagues, is the Island Marro /
                                                                         And

1613 The Iland Tidore

Aprill

7 And from that 2 leagues Tidore There is passage betweene these Islandes or on anie side of them without danger. Wee had sight of the two fflemmyes to the S. wardes of vs, plying after vs, Lattitude at noone ood. 35 minutes, winde westerlie.

Marro

8 Marro N by W some two miles of the bodie of it and one pointe N by E ½ pointe Easterlie and the other N W by N ½ pointe Westerlie, and the Pike of Tidore N by W, and opening the E. pointe of Tidore, and the W pointe of Bachian, they will beare the one from the other N and S. and the bodie of Marro W S W ½ pointe S ly, and the westerne parte of Tidore, that you shall see W by N. Looke well out, for in the faier wait, is along s'hole

A dangerous Shoald

which lieth even with the water at high water, the water shewing whitish and stretcheth N E and S W. Betweene Marro and Battachina. And having brought the pointes of the Islandes as aboueSaid then it wilbe E. of you at lowe water yet shall see it, for it ebbeth 6 foote, the tide setting 6 howers to the N ward, and 6 to the S ward. But keepe close to the Islandes, for there is noe feare. The Spaniards forte is on the E side of Tidore, where is

The Spaniardes fort on the Est side Tidore

deepe water shoare to. It fell suddenlie calme, soe that a great sea did sett vs in to the shoare. The forte made a shott at vs, but willinglie short. Wee aunswered with one to Seaboarde Then the forte made two more intending to strike vs, fix. 1 betwene our missen mast and auncient staff, thother betwixt mayne= mast, and foromast Then they shott a petir from the topp of the fort without sharpe wee aunswered that without. And then presentlie they sent of a boate with a Flagge of truce, the sea still setting vs vppon the shoare, noe winde nor grounde at 100 fath: soe that wee could sail it of not wait, two Gallies riding vnder the fforte. When theire boate was put from the shoare, they shott theire two chare petirs but without sharpe.

& tooke

They came fast a sterne our shipp. There were two Spaniardes souldiers of good ranck (knowne to Hernando the Spaniarde, whome wee tooke with vs from Bantam) sent from the Captaine Generall of the Shoare, Don Fernando Biseere, to knowe of what nation wee were, what wee came for and wherefore wee came not to an Anker vnder the kings fort. Wee requested them to come aboarde, the said they were commaunded to the contrarie, Wherefore I willed to lett downe wine and Breade vnto them in a stringe from the poope, which they fell to lustelie, in soe greate a shower of raine as wee had seene, yet would not enter the shipp. I returned aunswer that I was the subiect of the kings Maiestie

of

1613.   Tidore

April   8   of Greate Britaine, as by my Cullers they might well ~
             disterne. They said the Flemminges had manie times past by
             scott free, by shewing the like, which made them shoote the two
             shott with sharpe at vs, thinkinge vs to be Flemminges. I
             sent them worde, that my cominge was to doe the best good I
             could to the frindes of the kinge ma:tie of Spayne: but was
             not minded to anker heere but further a heade, where if it
             pleased Don Ferdinando to come aboarde hee should be ~
             welcome, with which aunswer they returned a shoare
             contented. Suddenlie it pleased God to graunt vs a Gale
             soe that wee stood alongest the shoare. The Captaine ~
             Generall sent off the Pilott Maior of the Galles Francisco
             Gomes a man of good presence, to bidd mee welcome, offering
             his assistaunce, to bringe vs into the best ankeringe place,
             vnder the fforte oreles wheare about the Island. Beinge
             darke hee brought vs to a place about 1½ leagues of the
             forte, whereas he said noe forte was and soe intreated
             after supper to be sett a shoare, for that the Captaine ~
             Generall would dispatch away letters to Ternata to y̌e
             Maister Del Campo, Don Jeronimo de Silua for resolutō
             in all poinites and soe departed.

         9   In the morninge before dait, findinge that wee were within
             com maunde of 8 peeces of ordinaunce, wee gott vpp our
             Anker, and removed a league further to the S'warde, where
             wee ridd in 35 fathom.

             Gomes the Pilott came aboarde with 2 Spaniards more
             of good fashion, whome I bidd kindlie welcome, soe that
             they tooke theire lodginge aboarde. They brought with them
             a Present of eatable commodities from theire Generall
             I returned the like to theires with proffer of all frindshipp
             and assistance that in mee laie, to supplie his wante with
             victuall or munition, and to accept of Cloaues for paym:t
             desiring speedie aunswer, for that I would not staie longe
             there.

             The two flemish shippes plied vs as if they would haue ~
             come to an anker by vs but afterwardes went and ridd at
Maracco a newe   theire newe forte Maracco.
forte of the Hol=
landers.   10   The Captaine Generall sent to request me to staie, and the
             next morninge hee would visitt me with the Sergeant
                                                              Maior

1613.   Tidore and Ternata

Aprill 10. Maior of Ternate, whoe was arived with a letter from
the maister Del Campo, givinge them leaue therby to trade
with me for diuers matters, and to content mee in what I
requested. wherefore I resolved a while longer to see what good
myght be donne.

11. Wee expected the Captaine Generall accordinge to promise,
and hearinge 9 peeces of ordinaunce to be shott out of the forte
provided for them, thinkinge verelie that they were cominge.
But it proved to be for the arivall of the prince of Tidore
whoe had bynn abroade in warr, and was nowe returned
with the heades of 100 Ternatanes, his forte beinge onelie
60 smale shott, two Brass Bases and 3 or 4 Fowlers, & &
havinge overthrowne Key Chilli sadang the kinge of
Ternata his sonne, whome the Flemminges had misorted
over from Ternate to Machian to keepe the countrie
people from sellinge of Cloaves to vs. ffor whome & &
returninge back towardes Ternata (after our departure)
the kinge of Tidoraes sonne, lyinge purposelie in waite, &
vppon sight of them the Tidorians keepinge themselves
behinde a pointe of land, sent out two smale Praws to fish
in theire waie, whome the Ternatanes espying did presentlie
give chase vnto. The fishermen caselie retire, the other
earnestlie pursue vntill before they once thought thereof,
they fell into theire enimies handes, Whoe spared not one
mann of 160. The prince of Ternata himself beinge one
of the number, whose heade the Conqueror brought to his
wife, whoe was sister to the prince of Ternata soe slayne,
Att theire first encounter, a Barrell of Powder which the
Prince had bought of vs at Machian tooke fier which
was the confusion and losse of them all, with the prince
was slaine one of his younger bretheren, and the kinge of
Geilolo. Towardes eveninge came aboarde vs the
Sergeant Maior of Ternata, and secretarie of State, with
the like complementes to those of the Tidorian officers, &
requestinge mee to come thether, and they would doe what
in them laie for mee, whereto I consented the rather because
it was in my waie.

12. The prince of Tidore sent vnto mee to excuse his hetherto not
visitinge of me, and to acquainte me, that hee had some store
of

1613.   Ternata
Aprill.   12   of Cloaues which I should haue, I thanked him and requested
                speedie dispatch, they promised mee to be aboarde againe before
                daie, wherefore to prevent all treacherie wee kept doble watch
                match in cock and all thinges in readinies / This Tidorian
                Prince being a verie resolute and valient souldier hauing o-
                performed manie dangerous exployts vppon the fflemynges
                and not longe since surprized one of theire shipps (being a man
                of warr) then ridinge not farr from this place /
                Before daie a Gallie (which the Spamards tould vs they expected)
                came over from Batta China and were neere vs in the darke
                before they were aware, wee haled her, they aunswered Spaniards
                and your frindes and soe made to the shoare with all speede, shee
                was but small of 14 oares on a side / Att noone, Lattitude 00.m 50.
                to the N ward of the Equinoctiall.

           13   Wee waied the winde N.E, and a current setting out of the S.ward
                passing by the forte wee gaue them 3. peeces which they required
                diverse Spaniards boarded vs with complements and the
                Printed man saininge, that if wee had staied but 24 howers
                longer wee should haue had good store of Cloaues, But wee
                rather thought they intended some treacherie against vs with
   4 Shipps of Holland theire Gallies, ffrigatte and Curra curraies, which by sudden
                departure wee thus prevented. Cominge about the westerpoint
                of Tidore wee had sight of the 4 Flemish shipps ridinge before
                theire forte of Maricco; One of them at sight of vs shott of a
                peece of Ordinaunce as wee supposed, to call theire people aboard
                to followe vs, wee steered directlie with the ffortresse of Ternata
                Cominge neere, shortned our sailes and lay by the Lee and shott of
                a peece towardes the towne without sharpe, which they readelie
                aunswered and sent of a souldier of good fashion, but to as little
                purpose as those of Tidore had donne/
                But litle winde our shipp sagged in and not ankoring, but at
                night a gale at S: wee stood into the sea, hauing lost much by the
                currant of that wee had gotten, finding it to sett to y S. ward/

           14   The winde at S.S.W wee steered N.N.W and at noone had Latt.
                1°.00.m wee had sight of a Gallie, wherefore wee cast about, but
                finding her to stand awaie went our course for Japan.
                But before wee parte further from this Moluccan coast, I think
                it not amisse to acquainte the reader with a fewe notes that I hold
                worthie of observance touching the trade and state of y Hands
                                                            Throughout

_1613_   Of the Moluca Ilands.

Aprill 14 Throughout all the Molucca Islandes, a Bahar of Cloaues doth waigh 200 Catties of that countrie, everie Cattie 3 pound 5 ounces, haberdepoize subtill. For which Bahar of Cloaues the Fleminges by theire perpetuall contract (as they terme it) giue 50 Royalls of 8. My selfe for more speedie obtayninge of ladinge yeelded to paie them 60 Royalls of 8. the Bahar, which increase of price made them soe forwarde to furnish vs, that had not the Fleminges by theire force overawed the nationalls, imprisoning and threatning them with death and keepinge watch and good guardes alongest the seacoast, I had in one moneth procured our full ladinge. The most of the Islandes Molucas doe beare store of Cloaves, those of note inhabited yeeld one yeare with another as followeth. vizt

		Baharrs
Ternate		1000
Machian		1090
Tidore		0900
Batchian		0300
Motuere		0600
Meau		0050
Batta China		0035
Totall		**3975**

Nota. 19 Catties Ternata makes 50 Catties Bantam

Everie thirde yeare is farr more fruitefull then either of the former two and is called the greate Monson. It is lamentable to see the ruines that civill warr hath bredd in those Islandes which as I vnderstand at my being there, beganne and continued in manner followinge. The Portugall at his first discouerie of them founde fierce warres betwixt the kinge of Ternate and the kinge of Tidore, vnder which two kinges all the other Islandes are either subiected, or confederated with one of them. The Portugall for the better setlinge of himselfe tooke parte with neither of them but pollitiquelie carrying himselfe kept both to be his frindes, and soe fortefied vppon the Islandes of Ternata and Tidore. Where (to the Portugalls greate advauntage) having the whole trade of Cloaves in theire owne handes, they domineered and bore themselfe swaie vntill the yeare 1605. wherein the Fleminges by force displaced them and planted himselfe. But soe weaklie and vnprovided for future danger that the next yeare the Spaniard (who whilest the Portugale remained there was ordered both by the Pope and kinge of Spaine not to meddle with them) came from the Philippinas, beate the fleminges out of the Islandes, tooke the kinge of Ternata prisoner, sent him to the Philippinas, and kept Ternata and Tidore vnder theire commaund

The Hollanders planted in the Moluccas. 1605

The

1613 Moluccas
Aprill. 14. The Fleminges since that time hath gotten footinge there againe, and at my beinge there, had built him these ffortes, vizt

Vpon the Island Ternata

They haue a fforte called Malayou, which hath 3 Bolwarkes and is walled rounde about /

Secondlie Tolouco which hath two Bolwarkes and a rounde Tower walled about /

Thirdlie Tacome which hath fower Bulwarkes and is walled about /

Vpon the Island Tydore

Marieco, which hath fower Bolwarkes /

Vpon the Island Machian

1. Tafasoa (the cheefe towne of the Island) where they haue 4 greate Bolwarkes walled about, 16 peeces of ordinaunce, and about on thowsand inhabitants of the naturalles /

2. Nafokia another towne where they haue two fortes walled about and another fort vppon the topp of a highe hill there, which sweeth the roade on the other side, and hath 5 or 6 peeces of ordmaunte /

3. Tabalola a towne where they haue two fortes walled 8 peeces of Ordmaunte, and the Inhabitantes heereof (as of the former) wnder theire comiaunde, this place is verie stronglie sittuated by nature /

Those of Nafokia, are esteemed noe good souldiers but are reported to take parte allwaies as neere as they can guesse it, with the strongest / But the naturalls of Tabalola which formerlie dwelt at Cayoa are accompted the best soldiers of the Maluca Islandes and are deadlie enimies to the Spaniarde and Portugalls and as wearie nowe of the Fleminges /

In these three fortes vppon Machian there were at my beinge heere 120 Holland soldiers viz. 80 Tafasoa, 30 Nofakia, and 10 Tabalola which garrison is with the least /

This Island Machian is the richest of Cloaues, of all the Malucca Islandes and according to the generall report of the Inhabitantes yeeldeth in the yeare of the greate Monson, aboue 1800 Baharrs of Cloaues.

Vpon

1613.
Aprill:

Moluccas

Vpon the Island Batchian

The Flemminges haue one greate Forte.

Vpon the Island Moteer.

They haue ffower Bulwarkes.

These civill warres haue soe wasted the nationalles, that a greate quantitie of Cloaues perish and rott vppon the grounde for want of gatheringe, neither is there anie likelihoode of peace to be made betwixt them vntill the one parte be vtterlie rooted out. Whereto the ffleminge and Spaniard giue all the waie they maye, for sittinge at ease in theire fortes they giue the nationalls leaue to ridd one another by cruell warr as aforesaide.

Thus leauinge them to theire warres, I will returne to our trafique and shewe in what manner wee traded with the nationalles for Cloaues which for the most parte was by barteringe, and exchangingy Cotten cloth of Cambaia and Coromandell for Cloaues. The sortes requested and prizes that they yielded at our beinge in the Moluccæ are as followeth. Vzt.

		Catties.
The seuerall sorts of Cambaian & Choromandell Cloth vendible heere	Candakeenes of Barochy	6.
	Candakeenes Papang or flatt	3.
	Selas or smale Baftas	7. & 8
	Patta chere Malayo	16.
	Dragam chere Malayo	16.
	Fine Cassas	12
	Course of that kinde	08.
	Betelhas or Tancoulos redd	44. & 48
	Sarassas chere Malayo	48 & 50
	Sarampouri	30.
	Chelles, Tapsiels and Matafons	20 & 24.
	White Cassas or Tancoulos	40 & 44

1613 From the Moluccas to Iapan.

April 14.

	Catties
Dongerijns the finest	12
Course of that kinde	08 & 10
Pouti castella	10
Ballachios the finest	30
Patta there Malayo of 2 Fathoms	08 & 10
Greate Potas, or long 4 Fathom	16
Parcallas white	12
Salalos ytam	12 & 14
Turias and tappe Turias	01 & 2
Patola of two fathoms	50 & 60

Those of 4 and one fathom accordinglie

Rice —— 28 poundes a Royall of 8.

Sagu which is a roote whereof the naturalls make theire breade and is theire cheefest foode throughout the whole countrie, It is sould in bunches and was worth then ¼ of a Royall of 8 a bunch

Velvetts, Sattens, Taffaties, and other stuffes of silke, of China are verie well requested heere

And this shall suffice for advise concerninge the Molucca Islandes

Wee sett saile for Iapan,

directing our Course to the Estward of the Philipinas, being a waie undiscovered by anie Christian, untill this present time.

———————

15. The winde at N.N.E wee steered W. by N. but y winde bearing to the S. wee steered N. sometimes E.ly, and sometimes W.ly but gott little ahead, verie much Rayne and subiect to calmes

16. Calme untill night, then a gale at W. wee steered N.N.W.

17. Morninge winde at E by S. steered N. but after variable & shiftinge

1613   The Iland Doy

Aprill

17. shifting to all the pointes of the Compasse, Towardes night wee had sight of land to the N: wardes/

18. Calme much rayne and contrarie windes, I therefore resolved to goe for the Island Saiem which was to the W. ward and there to staie and refresh vs till the Monson would permitt mee to proceede, But instantlie the winde came to the W, Soe that wee stood N and N. by E:

19. Little winde at W, wee continued our course N. by E, verie much raine, and extreame hott/

A Current to the Estward

20. Morninge calme and a continuall current, setting to the E: warde, which wee haue felt euer since our departure from Ternata, In the afternoone, the winde N. a gale, wee stoode to the W. warde to stemm the current/ In regarde of the N.ly windes subiect to calmes and the E.ly current wee stood in with a greate Island called Doy, to rest and refresh our selues/

Doy a greate Island &

21. Morninge wee were faire before the said Island neere the Nothern pointe being a lowe pointe stretchinge to the S: wardes wee stoode in E. by S. winde at N. by E. At noone the skiff was sent to search out a conuenient place to ride in, but the current did sett soe stronge, to the E: wardes as that wee could not gett ahead, onelie discouered a Bay verie large but it had a greate shoale lyinge of the Nothern pointe, halfe a leagui into the sea, and had 6o fathom, 2 mile of the shoare sand, but night approchinge, wee stoode off till morninge/

A greate shoald

22. After sunne sett, wee Ankered in the Baye in 24 fathom hauing had standinge in 56. 35. 26 and 24 fathom Ridinge against a highe greene hill with one tree standing in a pitt, In the topp thereof in forme of a summer howse halfe a leagui within the N pointe of the shoalds which is drie at lowe water, The trees on the topp of the Greene bearing E. and by N. And the two outward pointes of the land, one of them N: E and by N. and the other W and by S./

23. Wee sent a skiffe ashoare to seeke a conuenient place to water in and to pitch a Tent for the Companie, to defend them from the rayne/. They founde such a place right ouer against the shipp, together with a greate tracke of Deere and Swine, but noe signe of people, the countrey full of aboundaunce of Coker trees, Penang, Serye and Palmitas, and Fowle, flezant, hearnes, hennshawes &c/ I went ashoare the marchauntes with mee; A tent was sett vpp; Our Carpenter made false pitts verie artificiallie, to take Swine, Some fish and Fowle wee tooke, but with some labour, Some of the Companie staied all night on shoare, to looke to the Trapps, They had sight of many large Swine, but tooke none/   This daie

1613   The Iland Doy.

Aprill	24	This daie about halfe an hower after 7 in the morninge, the moone in the full was Eclipsed in the strangest manner that ever anie of vs had seene, beinge obscured three howers and a half before shee recovered her perfect light, which vnto vs was verie fearefull,
A strang Eclipse of the Moone		
	28	The Companie laboured to gett in wood and water, The Skiff sounded about the shoale and founde 10 and 12 fathom neere to it, heere wee had much rayne daie and night,
	29	And 30 were spent in getting aboarde our woode, whereof wee had greate store, some 20 tunne because at Japan wee vnderstood it is very deere, and this is as good billitinge as anie wee have in England,
May	1	The Skiffe sounded to the westerne point into the Bay and found verie deepe water, landing, they found the rayne of howses and texten Brasse Pans, soe that wee were of oppynion that the place had latelie bene inhabited, But the Inhabitantes by the warres himted from theire homes,
Doy the Northermost end of Gelola	12	Wee sett saile from this Iland Doy, being the N E most Island of Battachina or Gelola in the Molucas Latitude 2d 35 minute Variation 5d 20 minutes Ely, Havinge remained heere 20 daies, and are in number 71 persons, being at noone 14 leagues N and by E of the place where wee Anckored having steered out of the Bay N.W. and by N. then N. the winde at W. W.N.W. and W.S.W. and at present W. verie much raine, and the Moone 3 daies onely
	13	The shipps waye to noont N and by E 22 leagues wee steerd N the winde at W Variation 5d and 30 minutes Ely, with a stronge current setting to the E warde
	14	Latt 5d 26m way N by E 26 leagues winde W and current as aforesaid sleete weather
	15	Latt 5d 56m way N N E 14 leagues currant as formerlie
	16	Latt 7d 10m way Nly 27 leagues winde at S W and W rayne
	17	Latt 8d 22m way N 24 leagues winde S W but in the morninge at E with rayne
	18	Latt 9d 07m way N Ely 15 leagues winde at E and E N E verie sleete weather
	19	Latt 9d 41m way N 11½ leagues winde E and E N E
	20	Latt 10d 40m way N ½ pointe Wly 20 leagues winde E and N E with help of a current Nly

                                                                                                            21 Latt 11

1613 — Our course towards Iapan

May

21. Latt: 11°.36ᵐ, way N.N.W. 20 leagues, winde N.E.E. N.N.E. and N.E. by E. Starboard, tack aboarde.

22. Latt: 12°.39ᵐ, way N.N.W. 23 leagues, winde E.N.E. N.E. by E. and N.E.

23. Latt: 12°.57ᵐ, way N. by W. 6⅔ leagues, winde S.E. calme.

24. Latt: 13°.42ᵐ, way N. 15 leagues, winde S. by E. verie smooth water.

25. Latt: 15°.12ᵐ, way N. 30 leagues, winde S. wee steered N.W.ly.

Note. Nota, that wee finde these favourable windes in the full of the Moone.

26. Latt: 17°.6ᵐ, way N. 38 leagues, winde S. by W. S. and S.S.W. a continuall stiff gale, and smooth water.

27. Way N.E. 24 leagues, winde at W.N.W. and W. with rayne ~ thunder and lightninge.

28. Way N. 9 leagues, winde W. and W.N.W.

29. Latt: 19°.15ᵐ, way N. 9 leagues, winde N.E.E. W. W.N.W. and S. calme and gusts.

30. Latt: 20°.12ᵐ, way N. 20 leagues, winde at S.E. and E.S.E.

Variation 6ᵈ. Esterly. 31. Latt: 21°.35ᵐ, way N. by W. 30 leagues, winde E. and E. by N. Variation 6°.00ᵐ E'ly.

Iune

1. Wee passed the Tropick of Cancer, the Sunne our Zenith, wee could not observe, waie N. 40 leagues, winde at S.E. and S.E. by E. Variation 5°.25ᵐ E'ly.

The Isles Dos Reys Magos.

2. Latt: 25°.44ᵐ, way N. 44 leagues, winde S.E. and S.E. by S. & making accompte wee should haue seene the Ilandes Des Reys Magos about 8 of the clock in the morninge, but as yet see none. About 4 afternoone wee made land, being a verie lowe Iland bearinge N.W. about 3 leagues off. winde S.E. by E. and hauing it N.N.E. wee had sight of the highland, over the lowe land, there beinge many little Ilandes, to the number of 10 or 11. with broken grownde and breaches reachinge over to each Iland, soe that wee could discerne noe passage to the westwarde. At night wee tarkt of, tooke in our topp sailes, and lay close by in our courses all night. winde verie much at S.S.E. wee steered E. The Ilandes lie alongst E. N.E. and S.W.

3. Breake of daie wee stoode in for the land, beinge a highe Iland bearinge N.W. seeminge to bee a most plesant and fruitefull soile, as anie wee had seene since our cominge out of England, well peopled, and greate store of cattell. wee purposed to haue come to an ancker about the N.E. pointe, and soundinge had 60 fathom. Had sight of two boates

1613. The Isles Dos Reys Magos.

June:

3 Boates cominge off vnto vs wee vsed all the meanes wee could to speake with them, beinge desirous of a pilatt, and to knowe the name of the Island, the better to be assured where wee were. But the winde was soe forrible as that wee could not gett in, wherefore wee stoode awaie N.W. wee steered with it, and from thence had sight of another Island bearinge N.E. ½ a point E'ly some 8 or 9 leagues of and cominge vnder the westermost Island wee disterned certen rockes that laie off the shoare, about two miles. The one about water, and the netthermost vnderwater, and is a greate waie without the other, the sea breakinge vppon it. Then the land falleth awaie to the S: wardes rounde and neare to the pointe you shall open a steepe rock that is vppon the west side of the Island, resemblinge Charing crosse.
Then wee steered N.W. with an extreame gale at S. by W. and S.S.W. when wee had opened the Island and a current, setting to the S. ward. At 4 of the clock wee tooke in our sailes, and haled close vppon a tarke. The Island beinge about. 7. leagues N.W. of vs, waie to noone N.E. ½ a pointe E'ly. 16 leagues.

4 In the morninge verie much winde at S.S.W. with rayne, way N.W. of all night 6 leagues, At 7 wee bore vpp and steered awaie our course N. and at 10 the wether verie violent wee tooke in all our sailes and huld, having made since wee bore vpp a N. by W. way. 9. leagues, and about noone it brake vp, waie to this present. N.N.W. ¾ westerlie. 20 leagues. At 3 afternoone, wee sett our course, the winde at N.W. and N.W. by N: wee steered N.E. some 2 howers then calme and rayne, Variation at sunne settinge 4°. 40 minutes. E'ly.

Variation 4°.
40 minutes E'ly

5 Way W. by N. 4 ½ leagues, winde N.N.E. wee steered N.W. starboarde tarke. Variation. 4°. 42 minutes.

6 way N.N.W. 9 leagues, winde E.N.E. N.E. by N. and N.E. by. E. little winde much raine. Variation. 4°. 19 m. E'ly At night the winde at E. and E.S.E.

7 waie N.E. by N. 16 leagues winde at S.E. and S.S.W. then wee steered awaie awaie N.E. by N. supposinge to be of Ionan 28. or 30. leagues

8 In the morninge wee had sight of a high rounde Island bearinge E. 6 leagues of with divers other Islandes risinge in 6. or 7 partes bearing W. 5 or 6 leagues of having made to this noone 22 leagues N.E by N. winde at S.S.W. a stiff gale Then wee haled over N.W. with another Island which wee founde to be fower in
unmber

1613. The Iland Xima or Mashma.
June   8 Number, being barren, and manie piked rockes, then wee
          steered N: by E: the winde at S: by W: about 3 of the clock wee
          had sight of an Island with 3 hills, like 3 runde suger loaves,
          bearinge E. by S: 5 leagues/ At 5 of the clock wee had sight of
          an Island risinge in two partes bearing N.N.E: the Norther end
          being an highe steeped upright pointe, the lande fallinge awaie
          to the E: ward, N.E: and at 6. of the clock the bodie of it did beare
          E. 1½ league of, the winde W, wee stood of uppon a tack N.N.W/

       9 In the morninge wee had sight of land bearinge N.N.E: and 6.
          greate Islandes on a ranke, from the Island wee descried
          yester night. N.E: and S.W. and at the nethermost ende of them all,
          many smale rockes and hummockes, and in the Bay to the E:ward
Xima or Mash= of the hummockes wee sawe a high land bearinge E: E. by S: and
  =ma.   E.S.E: which is the Island called Xima In the platts, But by the
          naturalles Mashma and the Island aforesaide N.N.E: is called
          Seque or Amaxay. It lieth E. by N: and W by S: with manie
          smale Islandes and rockes on the Sotherne side of them, And is
          distant from the Island with the steepe pointe (which wee did see
          the 8 daie) S.S.W. 12 leagues the winde calme all night, yet wee
          gott to the N: warde, as wee supposed, by the helpe of a current,
          or tide/

      10 Breake of daie, the outermost land to the W: warde did beare N.
          by E. 10 leagues of, the winde at N.E. by N: at 9. a gale at S: wee
          steered N. by W, and had sight of two hummockes without the point
          Then wee steered N.N.W. and soone after came 4 greate fisher boats
          aboarde about 5 tunnes apeece in burthen, they sailed without saile
          which stood like a stiff saile and sculd with 4 oares on a side, there
An excellent oares restinge uppon a pynn fastened on the topp of the boates side,
kinde of oares the heade of which pynn was soe lett into the middle parte of the
          oare, that the oare did hainge in his iust peaze, soe that the labo:r
          of the rower is much lesse then otherwise it must be, yet doe they
          make farr greater speede then our people, with rowinge and
          performe their worke standinge as ours doe sittinge soe that they
          take the lesse roome They tould us that wee went before the
Nagasague. entrannce to Nangasaque, bearing N.N.E: and the Straights
          of Arima, N.E. by N: and the highe hill which wee did see
          yesterdaie is uppon the Island called Yzideke which maketh the
          Straughtes of Arima, where at the Northermost end is good ridinge,
          and at the S: end is the goinge into Cochinoch./
                                                            Co.

1613 Firando in Iapan

June. 10 To this noone wee haue made a N wait 6 leagues, wee agreed with two of the maisters of the fisherboates for 30 R° of 8. a peece in money and rise for theire foode, to platt vs into Firando, which agreiment made, theire people entred our shipp and performed voluntarilie theire laboure as readelie as any of our marrinners. Wee steered N by W, the pilatts makinge attompt to be 30 leagues of Firando. One of the fower boates which came aboarde vs did belonge to the Portugalls liuinge at Langasaque and were newe Christians and thought that our shipp had bene the Maucau shipp, but findinge the contrarie would vppon not intreatie staie, but made hast back agayne to aduize them.

Wee ariued within half a league of Firando

11 About 3 in the afternoone wee came to an anker half a league short of Firando, the tide soe spent that wee could not yett further in. Soone after, was visited by the old kinge Foyne Sama and his nephewe Tone-sama Gouernour then of the Island vnder the ould kinge. They were attended with 40 boates or gallies rowed some with 10 some with 15 oares on a side. When they drewe nere to the shipp, the kinge commaunded all but the two where in himself and his nephewe were to fall asterne and they onelie entred the shipp, both of them in Silke gownes, guirt to them with a shirte, and a paier of breethes of flaxen cloth next theire bodies, each of them had two Cattans or swordes of that countrei by his side, the one of half a yarde longe thother about ¼. They weare not banded, The foreparte of theire headed, were shauen to the crowne, and the rest of theire heare, which was verie longe was gathered togeather and bounde vppon a knott behinde, wearinge neither hatt nor Turbant, but bareheaded. The kinge was aged about 72 yeares, his nephewe or Graundchild, that gouerned vnder him was about 22 yeres old, and either of them had his gouerno[r] with him whoo had commaunde ouer theire slaues as they appointed him. Theire manner and curtesie in salutinge was this. Virst in presence of him whome they are to salute, they putt of theire shooes (stockinges they weare noone) and then clapping theire right hand within theire left, they putt them downe towardes theire knees, and soe waggyinge or mouinge of theire handes a little to and fro, they stoopinge steppe with small steppes sideling from the partie saluted, and cry Augh Augh fledd

1613 Firando in Iapan

Iune 11 I ledd them into my Cabbyn, where I had prepared a Banckett for them and a good consorte off Musique, which much delighted them, they badd me welcome and promised me intertainement. I delivered our Kinges lres to the king of Firando, which hee receaved with greate ioye, saying hee would not open it, till Ange came whoe could interprett the same unto him. This Ange is in theire language a Pilott, being one William Adams an Englishman, whoe passing with a Flemminge through the S' Sea by mutenie and disorder off the mariners, shee remained in that countrie, and was seased uppon by the Emperoʳ about 12 yeares before. The kinge having staied aboarde about an hower and halfe, tooke his leave, Hee was not sooner ashoare, but all his nobilitie attended with a multitude off souldiers, entred the shipp, everie mann of worth brought his Present with him, some venison, some wildefowle, some wild boare the largest and fattest that ever anie of vs had seene, some fruites, fish &c̃ They much admired our shipp and made as if they had never seene it sufficientlie. But being pestered with the number of these visitors I sent to the kinge, requesting him that order might be taken to remove them, And to prevent all inconvenients that might happen. Whereuppon hee sent a Gardian being a principall mann of his owne Guarde, with charge to remaine and lie aboarde, that not iniurie might be offred unto vs, and caused a proclamation to be made in the Towne to the same effect. The same night Henrick Brower, captaine of the Dutch Factorie there, came aboarde to visitt mee, or rather to see what passed betweene the kinge and vs, This daie I writt to mʳ Adams, beinge then at Edoo, which is neere neere 300 leagues from Firando, to lett him understand off my arivall, King Foyn sent it awaie the next daie, by his Admirall of his Gallies to Osackey, the first porte of note, uppon the cheef Island, and then by post upp into the land to Edoo, Giving the Emperour likewise to understand of our being heere and cause thereof.

12 In the morninge there was brought aboarde, such aboundance off fish and fot theape as wee could desire, wee waied, and sett saile for the roade, The king sent at the least threescore greate Boates or Gallies verie well manned to bringe vs into the Harbor, I doubted what the cause of theire coming might be And.

1613   Firando in Iapan.

June   12   And was sending of the skiff to comaunde them not to come neere the shipp, but the kinge being the headmost weaved with his handkercher, and willed the rest to attend, and himself comnige aboarde, tould me that hee had commaunded them to toa our shipp in about a pointe, some what dangerous, by reason of the force of the tide which was such, that having a stiff gale of winde yet wee could not stemm it And comminge into the Eddy wee should haue bene sett vppon the Rockes. Soe wee sent hawsers aboarde them and they fell to worke. In the meane while the king did breake his fast with me, being at an Ancker. I would haue requited the people for theire paines, but the kinge would not suffer them to take anie thinge. Wee anckored before the towne in 5 fathom soe neere the shoare, that wee might talke to the people in theire howses.

Wee anckored before the Towne.

Wee saluted the towne with 9 peeces of Ordnaunce, but were not annswered, for they haue noe ordnaunce heere nor anie forte but Barricados, onelie for small shott. Our groinde heere was oaze. Divers noblemenn came to bidd me welcome whereof two were of extraordinarie accompt, called Nabusane and Simmadone, whoe were verie well entertained, and at parting held verie great state, one staying aboarde whilest the other were landed, Theire children and theef followers in the like manner. There came continuallie such a worle of people aboarde both menn and women, as that wee were not able to goe vppon the deckes. Rounde about the shipp was furnished with boates full of people, as mirmg much the heade and sterne of our Shipp.

I gaue leave to divers women of the better sorte to come into my Cabyn (where the Picture of Venus, with her sonne Cupid did hange some what wantonlie, sett out in a large frame, they thinking it to be our Ladie and her Sonne, fell downe and worshipped it, with shewes of greate devotion, telling me in a whispering manner (that some of theire owne companions which were not soe, might not heare) that they were Christianos, whereby wee perceaued them to be Christians converted by the Portugall Jesuites.

The kingt came aboarde againe and brought 4 theef women with him, they were attired in Gownes of silke clapt the one skirt over the other and soe guirt to them, bare legged, onelie a paire of half Buskins bounde with silke Ribband about theire insteps. Theire hayer verie black and verie long, tied vpp in a knott vpon the

1613   Firando in Iapan.

June

12. the Crowne in a comelie manner, theire heade noe way shaven
as the mennś were, They were well facedhanded, and footed theire
skynne, and white, but wantinge tallness which they amended by arte,
Off stature lowe, but verie fatt, verie curteous in behaviour, not
ignorant of the respect to be given unto persons accordinge to theire
fashion. The king requested that none might staie in the Cabbyn
save my self, and my Linguist, whoe was borne in Iapan, and was
brought from Bantam in our shipp thither, being well skild in ye
Mallayan tongue, wherein hee delivered me what the kinge spake
unto him in the Iapan language, The kinges women seemed to be
somewhat bashfull, but hee willed them to be frolick. They singe
diverse songes and plaid uppon certen Instruments (whereof one
did much resemble our Lute, being bellied like it but longer in the
neck, and fretted like ours, but had onelie 4 gutt stringes. Theire
fingeringe with the left hand like ours, verie nimblie, but the right
hand striketh with an Ivorie boane, as wee use to plaie on a
Cittern with a quill,

They delighted themselves verie much with theire musique, keeping
time with theire handes, playing and singinge by booke, prickt on
lyne and space, resemblinge much ours heere,

I feasted them and presented them with divers English commodities
and soe after some two howers staie, they returned, I moved the kinge
for a howse which hee readelie graunted, and tooke two of the
marchaunts alonge with him, and shewed them 3 or 4 howses,
willing them to take theire choice, paying the owners as they
could agree.

13. I went ashoare attended uppon by the marchaunts and
principall officers, and delivered the Presents to the kinge
amountinge to the value of 140.li or thereabouts, which hee
received with verie greate kindenes, feasting me and my whole
Companie with diverse sortes of powdred wilde fowle and fruites,
And callinge for a standing cupp (which was one of the Presents
then delivered him) hee caused it to be filled with his countrie wine
which is distilled out of Rice, and is as stronge as our Aqua vitæ
And albeit the cupp held uppwards of a pinte and a halfe,
Notwithstandinge takinge the Cupp in his hand, hee sould mee
hee would drincke it all off, for a health to the king of England,
and soe did my self, and all his Nobles doinge the like. And where
as in the roome where the kinge was, there was onelie my self and
the Cape Marchaunt (the rest of the companie being in another
roome) the king commaunded his Secretarie to goe out unto
them

1613   Firando in Iapan.
June

them, and see that everie one of them did pledge the health. The kinge
and his nobles did sitt at meate crosse legged vppon matts after
the Turkie fashion. The matts all thicke edged, some with cloth of gould,
some with velvett, satten, and damaske/

14 And 15th wee spent with giuinge of Presentes, &c.

16 I conchuded with captaine Audassee, captaine of the China
quarter heere, for his howse to paie 95 Royalls of 8 for the Monson
of 6 monethes, hee to repaire it at present, and wee to repaier it
heereafter and alter what wee pleased, hee to furnish all convenient
roomes with matts according to the fashion of theire countrie/

This daie our shipp was soe pestered with people, as that I was
enforced to send to the kinge for a Guardian to cleere them out, many
thinges beinge stolne, but I more doubted our people then the o o
naturalles/ There came in a fleminge in one of the countrie boates
which had bene at the Island Mashma where hee had sould good store
of pepper, Broade cloth, and Elephants teeth, but would not be
knowne vnto vs to haue sould anie thinge, yet brought nothinge
back in the boate with him; But the Japans his watermen tould
vs the truth. viz.t that hee had sould good quantitie of Goods at a
mart there, and returned Barres of Silver, which they kept verie
secrettlie/

21 The ould kinge came aboarde agayne and brought with him diverse
women to be frolick. These woemen were actors of Commedies, w.ch
passe there from Island to Island to plaie, as our plaiers doe heere
from Towne to towne, hauinge severall shiftes of apparell for the
better grace of the matter acted, which for the most parte are of
love and warr, and such like. These woemen are as the slaves of one
mann, who putteth a price what euerie man shall paie that hath to
doe with them, more then which hee is not to take vppon paine of
death, in case the partie iniured shall complaine, It is left to his
owne discrition to prize her at first, but rise hee cannot afterwarde
but fall hee maye/ Neither doth the partie bargayne with the
wench, but with hermaister, whose commaunde shee is to obeye

The greatest of theire nobilitie travelling should it not disgrace to
send for these Panders to theire Inne, and doe compounde with them
for theire wenches, either to fill theire drinck at table (for all men of
anie ranck haue theire drinck filled to them by women) or otherwise
to haue the vse of them

When anie of these Pandars dye (though in theire life time they were
receaued into companie of the best, yet nowe as vnworthie to rest
amougest the worst) They are bridled with a bridell made of strawe
as yet would bridle a horse, and in the clothes they died in are
                                                                  dragged

1613. Firando in Japan.

June 23. Dragged through the streetes into the fieldes and there cast vppon a dunghill, for dogges and fowles to devowre/

23. Wee had newes of two China Junckes arived at Langasaque laden wt suger, by him wee vnderstood that the Emperour of China had then latelie put to death 5000 persons for tradinge out of the Cuntrie co[n]trarie to his edict confiscatinge all theire goodes/ Notwithstandinge hope of proffitt entired these men to put it in hazard hauing bribed the newe Tungauas and officers vppon the scaroste, which vppon the execution of the former, were placed in theire steedes/

29. A Soma or Junck of the Flemminges arived at Langasaque from Syam laden with Brasill wood and Skinnes of all sortes wherein it was said that there were English men but proved to be Flemminges, for that before our cuming they passed generallie by the name of English men. For our English nation hath beene longe knowne by report amongst them, but much scandalized by the Portugall Jesuites, as pirates and robbers vppon the seas/ soe that the naturalles haue a songe which they call the English crosonia shewinge howe the English doe take the Spanish shipped, which they (singing) doe at likewise in gesture with theire Cattans by theire sides, wt which songe and actinge they terrifie and scare theire children as the french sometimes did theires with the name of the Lo: Talbott.

The Hollenders formerlie passed vnder the name of Englishmen/

Julie 1. Two of our Companie happened to quarrell the one with the other, and were verie likelie to haue gone into the field, to the endangerment of vs all. for it is a custome heere, that whoe soever drawes a weapon in anger, all though hee doe noe harme there with, hee is presentlie cutt in peeces/ And doinge but smale hurte, not onelie themselues are soe executed, but theire whole generation, and if it be thus with the naturalls themselues, strangers were best to beware howe they presume vppon anie priviledge or hope of favour/

Nota 2. I went ashoare to keepe howse in Firando the howsehould consistinge of 26 persons/ Note that at our cuminge wee founde Broadeclothes of 15. or 16 pound a cloth to be soulde by the Dutch in Firando for 40 Royalls of 8, which is 8 pounde sterling the Matt, which Matt is 2¼ yardes/ But desirous to keepe vp the price of our cloth and hearing that the Dutch had greate store there, I had conference with Brower captaine of theire ffactorie to this effect, That betwixt vs wee should sett rates vppon such clothes as both of vs had and neither of vs in anie wise to sell vnder the price agreed vppon, for performance whereof I proferedd to enter into bond to him In the morninge hee seemed to approve hereof, but before night sent worde that hee disliked it excusinge himself that he had noe warrant from his Maisters to make any such agreement/

Tho.

1613.   Firando in Japan.

Iulie: 2 The next morninge hee shypped away good store of cloath to divers Islandes, rating them at base pritts viz.t at 20. 18 and 16. Royalls the matt, that hee might procure the more speedie dispatch of his owne and glutt the place before the cominge of ourb &c. Bantam Pepper vngarbled which cost at Bantam 1¾ Royalls of 8 the sack, was worth heereat our cominge 10 Tayes the Peecull, which is 100 Catties, making English 130 pounde subtill. A Taye is 5 s.d. sterlinge with them, A Royall of 8 is worth there in ordinarie payement but 7 Mass, which is 3 s. vj d. sterlinge. ffor Mass is ab a Royall of Plate.

	Tayes.
Tynne the Peecull	0 3 0
Ellephants teeth the Peecull	0 8 0
Iran cast peeces the Peecull	0 0 6
Powder the Peecull	0 2 3
Aloes socotrina the Cattie	0 0 6
Fowling Peeces the peece	0 2 0

Callico and such like comodities of Choromandell, and of the Guzaratts ab they are in goodnes.

7 The kinge of the Island Goto, not farr from Firando, came to visitt king Foyne, saying that hee had heard of an excellent English shipp arived in his dominions, which hee greatlie desired to see and got aboarde of. King Foyne intreated mee that hee might be admitted, for that hee was an especiall frinde of his. Soe hee was well entertained aboarde, bankitted and had divers peeces shott of at his departure. Which hee verie kindelie accepted, and tould mee that hee should be right gladd to live to see some of our nation to come to his Islands, whether they should be hartelie wellcome.

the kinge of Goto desirous of our men to come into his kingdome.

8 Three Japons were executed viz.t 2 men, and one woman The cause was this The woman (none of the honestest) her husband being travelled from home shee appointed these two theire severall howers to repaire vnto her for a match. The latter man not knowing of the former, and thinking the time to longe, comme in before the hower appointed, founde the first man in the place where hee intended to haue bent wherewith hee whipt out his Cattan and wounded both of them verie sorelie, ab having verie neere hewen the Chyne of the mans back in two. But as well as hee might hee cleered himself of the woman and recovering his Cattan wounded the other, The streete taking notice of the fray

Execution

1613.   Firando in Iapan.

Iulie

8 A fray forthwith seased vppon them, ledd them a side, and acquain=ted kinge Foyne therewith, and sent to knowe his pleasure (for ac-cordinge to his will the partie is executed) whoe presentlie gaue order that they should cutt off theire heades, which was donne, every mann that listed (as verie many did) came to trie the sharpenesse of theire Cattans vppon the corpes, soe that before they left off, they had hewen them all three into peeces, as smale as a mans hand, and yet notwithstandinge did not then giue over, But placinge the peeces one vppon another, would trie howe manie of them they could strike throughe at a blowe, And the peeces are left for the fforwles to devowre.

To steale an=
others slaue is
death.

10 Three more were executed, as the former, for stealing of a woman from Firando, and sellinge her at Langasacque long since, two of them were Brethren, and the other a sharer with them. When anie are to be executed, they are ledd forth of the towne in this manner. There goeth first one with a Pickax, next followeth another with a shovell for to make his graue, the thirde man beareth a smale Table, wherein is written the parties offence, which Table is afterwards sett vpp vppon a poste, on the Graue where hee is buried, Then fourth is the partie to be executed, his handes bound behinde him with a silken twande, hauing a little banner of paper (much resemblinge our windo vanes) whereon is likewise written his offence. The Executioner followeth, whoe next with his Cattan by his side, houldinge in his handes the Corde wherewith the offender is bounde, On either side of the executioner goeth a souldier with his Pike, the head thereof restinge on the shoulder of the partie appointed to suffer, to staye him from attemptinge to escape. In this verie manner I sawe one ledd to execution whoe went soe resolutlie and without all appearannce of feare of death that I could not but much admire him, never havinge seene the like in Christendome. The offence for which hee suffred, was for stealing of a bagg of Rice of the value of i s vj d from his neighbour, whose howse was then on fire.

The manner of
theire goinge to
Execution

11 There arived at Langesacque three China Iunckes laden with silkes.

19 The ould king Foyne intreated me for a peere of Poldauis, which I sent him, hee caused it presentlie to be made into Coates which hee (notwithstandinge that hee was a kinge and of that greatt age and famed to be the worthiest souldior of all Iapan for his vallor and seruice in the Corean warrs) did weare next his skynne, and some parte thereof was made into handkerchers which hee dailie vsed.

20 A Soma or Iunck cominge from Cochinchina arrived at Langasacque, laden with silkes and Beniamine excellent steere and ritch.

1613   Firando in Iapan.

Iulie.   20   Pith &c

       29   Mr Adams arrived at Firando, havinge byn 17 daies on the waie comminge from Sorongo, wee havinge staied theire for his cominge 48 daies. After that I had frindlilie entertained him, I conferred with him in the presence of the marchauntes, touchinge the incouragement hee could giue of trade in these partes, hee aunswered that it was not allwaies alike, but sometimes better, and sometimes worse, yet doubted not but wee should doe aswell as others, givinge admirable commendations of the countrie, as much affected thereunto.

       30   In the morninge one of the younge kinges governor was by his order cutt in peeces in the streete, for beinge (as it was thought) too familier with his mother, a slave of his died with him, for indeauouringe to defend his master.

An intention of ye Spaniarde to discouer to the N. ward of Japan

           This daie there came to Firando ten Spaniardes of Mr Adames his acquaintance to desire passage in our shipp to Bantam. These Spaniardes had bene belonginge to a Spanish gentleman theire Generall whoe about a yeare past went come vppon the kinge of Spaines charge) from Noua Hispania to discouer to the N. wardes of Japan and arivinge at Edoo, attendinge the Monson to goe to the N. ward which beginneth in the ende of Maye, his Companie (whereof these were two) mutined against him, everie man takinge his owne waie, leavinge the shipp vtterlie vnmanned, Wherefore I thought it best to keepe them out of my shipp.

August. 3   Kinge Foyne sent to knowe of what Bulke our kinges Present to the Emperour was, alsoe what number of people I would take with mee, for that hee would provide accordinglie for my goinge vpp in good fashion, both for Barke, Horses, and Pallanchin.

           This daie I caused the Presents to be soarted, that were to be given to the Emperour, and to those of office and esteeme aboute him. vizt.

	li. s. d.
To Ogoshosama the Emperour to ye value of	87. 7. 6
To Shongosama the Emperors sonne	43. 15.
To Codskedona the Emperours Secretarie	15. 17. 6
To Saddadona the Emperours sonnes Secretary	14. 03 4
To Frocora Iuga Judge of Meaco	04. 10. 0
To Fongo dona Admirall of Orunga	03. 10. 0
To Goto Shozauero the Mintmaister	11. 0. 0
Totall —	180. 03 10

Kinge

1613　　　　　　　The towne of Fuccate.

August. 7

King Foyne furnished mee with a proper Gally of his owne, rowed with 25 oares on a side and 60 men which I did fitt vpp in a verie comelie manner with waste clothes, Ensigne, and all other necessaries. And having taken my leave of the king, I went and remained aboarde the shipp, to sett all thinges in order before my departure, which donne and remembrances left with the Master and Cape Marchant for the well govermente of the shipp and house ashoare during my absence, taking with me, 10 English and 9 others besides the former 60, which were onlie to attend the Gallie.

My setting forward towards the Emperours Courte

I departed from Firando towardes the Emperours Court, wee were rowed through and amongest divers Isslandes, all which or ye most of them, were well inhabited, and divers proper townes built vppon them, whereof one called Fuccate, hath a verie stronge Castell built of ffreestone but not Ordinaunce nor souldiers therein. It hath a ditch about 5 fathom deepe, and twise as broade, rounde about it with a drawe bridge, kept all in verie good repaire, I did land and dyne theire in the Towne, the tide and winde soe stronge against vs as that wee could not passe. The towne seemed to be as greate as London is within the walles, well built and even, Soe as you maie see from one end of the streete to the other. The place exceeding[l]ie peopled verie civill and curteous. Onelie that at or landinge and being heere in Fuccate, and soe through the whole country whether soever wee came, the boies, children, and worser sorte of idle people would gather about and follow alonge after vs crying Core Core cocore ware, that is to saie, you Coreans with false harted wondringe, hoopinge, hallowing and makinge such a noise about vs that wee could scarce lie heare one another speake, sometimes throwing stones at vs (but that not in many townes) yet the clamore and crying after vs was everie wheare alike, none reproving them for it.

The best advise that I can give those whoe heereafter shall come there, is, that they passe on without regarding those idle rable[m]t, and in soe doing they shall finde their eares onlie troubled.

Women with theire household that liuein botes vpon the water

All alongest this coast and soe vpp to Ozaca, wee founde Women divers that lived with theire howsehold and familie vppon the water in boates, as in Holand they doe the like. These women would catch fish by diving which by nett and lynes they missed, and that in 8 fathom deepe, Theire cives by continuall divinge doe growe as redd as blood, whereby you maie knowe a diving woman from another woman.

Wee were two daies rowing from Firando to Fuccate, passinge onwardes of our iourney about 8 or 10 leagues on the side of the Straightes

1613   The cittie Ozaca!

August 7   Straightes of Xemina-seque wee founde a greatt towne
           where there laie in a docke a Junck of 800 or 1000 tunnes of
           burthen, sheathed all with Jron with a guarde appointed to kepe
           her from firinge and treatherie, Shee was built in a verie home-
           ly fashion, much like that which discribeth Noahs Arck vnto vs,
           The naturalls toulde vs that shee served to transporte souldiers into
           anie of the Islandes, if rebellion or warres should happen,
           Wee founde nothinge extraordinarie after wee had passed the
Osaca   Straightes of Xemina-seque, vntill wee came to Osaca where
     27.   wee arrived the 27 daie of August, our Gallie could not come
           neere the towne by 6 miles where another smaller vessell mett vs
           wherein came the Goodman or Ost of the howse, where wee laye
           in Osaca, and brought a banckett with him of wine and salt fruits
           to entertaine me with, The boate havinge a saste made to the
           Mast head was drawne by men, as our Barges are from London
           westward, Wee founde Osaca to be a verie greate towne as
           greate as London within the walles with many faire Timber
           bridges of a greate height, servinge to passe over a River there as
           wide as the Thames at London, some faire howses we founde
           there, but not manie. It is one of the chiefe seaportes of all
           Japan, havinge a Castell in it marveilous large and stronge with
           verie deepe trenches about it and manie drawe bridges with
           Gates plated with yron, The Castell is built all of freestone,
           with Bulworkes and battlementes with loope holes for smale
           shott and arrowes, and divers passages for to cast stones vppon
           the assaylantes, The walles are at the least 6 or 7 yardes thick,
           all (as I saide) of freestone without any fillinge in the inwarde
           parte, with Curiuetries (as they reported vnto me, The stones
           are greate, of an excellent quarrie and are cutt soe exactlie to
           fitt the place where they are laide, that noe morter is vsed, but
           onelie earth cast betweene to fill vpp voide crevises if any be/
           In this Castell did Dwell at our beinge there the sonne of
The sonne of   Tiqua:sama who being an Infant at the time of his fathers
Tiqua:sama.   decease was left to the Government and Education of fower,
           whereof Ogosho:sama the nowe Emperour was one, and these,
           The other 3 desirous of Soveraignety each for his particuler,
           and repulsed by Ogosho-sama were for theire owne safetie
           forced to take vpp Armes wherein fortune favouring Ogosho-sama
           at the triall in fielde, two of them beinge slayne, the thirde was
           gladd to save himselfe by flight, Hee being conquerour,
           attempted that which formerlie (as it is thought, he never
                                                                    Drempt

1613   The cittie Fushimi.

August 27 dreampt of, and proclaimed himselfe Emperoure, and seasinge
           vppon the true heyre, married him vnto his daughter, as the
           onelie meanes to worke a perfett reconcilement consyninge the
           younge married coople to live within the Castell of Osaca,
           attended onelie with such as had bene brought vpp from their
           Cradells by Ogosho-sama, not knowinge any other father (as
           it were) then him, soe that by theire intelligence hee could at
           all times vnderstande what passed there, and accordinglie
           rule him.

S'acay.   Right over against Osaca, on the other side of the river, lieth
           another greate towne called S'acay but not soe bigge as Osaca
           yet it is a towne of greate trade, for all the Ilandes thereaboute/

        28 At night having left musters and prizes of our comodities
           with our Caste wee parted from Osaca by Barck towarde
Fushimi.   Fushimi, where wee arived,

        29 at night, wee founde heere a garrison of 3000 souldiers mayn-
           =teyned by the Emperour, to keepe Miaco and Osaca in subiection
           The garrison is shifted everie three yeares which chainge
           happened to be at our beinge there, soe that wee sawe the old
           Band, march awaie and the newe enter, in most souldier like
           manner, marchinge 5 abrest, and to everie 10 fyles an officer
           which is called a captaine of 50, and kept them continuallie in
           verie good order. ffirst theire shott, viz.t Caliuers, (for Muskets
           they haue none, neither will they vse any) then followed Pikes,
           next Swordes or Cattanes & Targetts, then Bowes and
           Arrowes, next those weapons resembling most a Welsh hooke,
           called Waggadashes. Then Caliuers againe and soe as
           formerlie, without any Ensigne or Collors, neither had they
           anie drumes or other Musicall Instrumentes for warr.
           The first file of the Cattanes and Targetts, had silver
           Scabardes to theire Cattans and the last file, which was next
           to the Captaine, had theire scabbardes of Gould.

           The Companies consisted of divers numbers, some 500, some 300
           some 150. In the middest of everie companie were 3 horses
           verie richlie trapped and furnished with saddles well sett out
           some covered with costlie furres, some with velvett, some with
           staimett broadcloth everie horse had 3 slaues to attend him, ledd
           with silken halters, theire eyes covered with lether covers. After
           everie troope followed the Captaine on horseback, his Bedd
           and other necessaries were laide vppon his owne horse
                                                                equally

1613.   Fushimi.

August 29

equallie peazed, on either side over the same, was spredd a rovering off redd felt off China, whereupon the ∞ ∞ Captaine did sitt crosse legged, as iff hee had sitt betweyt a roople off pannicks, And for those that were antient or otherwise weake backt, they had a staff artifitiallie fyxed vnto the Pannell, that the rider might rest himselfe and leant backroardes against it, as iff hee were sittinge in a Chaier. The captaine Generall of this Garrison wee mett two daies after the meetinge with the first troope, (havinge still in the meane time mett some of these companies as wee passed alonge, sometimes one league, sometimes 2 leagues distant one from another) Wee marched in verie greate State beyond that the others did, ffor the seconde troope was more richlie sett out in theire Armies then the first, and the thirde then the second, and soe everie one better then the other, vntill it came vnto this the last best off all) Hee hunted and hawked all the waie, havinge his owne hyundes and hawkes alonge with him, The hawkes beinge hooded and luxed as ourts are, His horses for his owne saddle beinge six in number, richlie trapped,

Theire Horses — Theire horses are not tall but of the size of our midling nagges, shortt and well trust, small headed, and verie full off mettle, in my opinion, farr excellinge the Spanish Jennett in pride and stomark

Hee had his Pallankein carried before him, the Inside off Crimson velvett and 6 men appointed to carrie it, two at a time, Such good order was taken for the ∞ passing and providinge for of these 3000 souldiers, that not manie either travillinge or inhabitinge vppon the wayes where they lodged, was anie waie iniured by them but theire fullie entertained them as other theire Guestes, because they paid for what they tooke as all others men did Everie towne and village vppon the waie beinge well fitted with Cookes and virtuallinge howses, where they might at an instant haue what they needed and dietted themselues, from a penny English a meale to 18 a meale The diett vsed generallie throughe the countrey is Rice of divers sortes, one better then another, as of our wheate and corne there, the whitest accompted the best, which they vse insteede of breade, fish fresh and salted

some

1613		Fushimi
August	29	Some pickeled wildfowle, Duck, Mallard, Teale, Goose, Phesant, Partridge, Quaile, and divers others which they doe powder and put vpp in pickle, Of Henns they haue greate store, as likewise of Deere both redd and fallowe, wilde bores, hares, Goates, kyne &c Of these they haue plentie, butter they make none, neither will

blood — they eate any milke, because they hould it to be as bloode Nor tame beastes /

Of tame swyne and pigges they haue greate aboundaunce, wheate they haue as good as anie of ours, being redd, They plowe both with Oxen and horse, as wee doe heere / At our beinge there wee bought henns and phesants of the best for ij d apeece, pigges verie fatt and large vij d apeece, a fatt hogge vs, a good beeffe, such as o~ welch runts, at xxjs. A Goate ijs. rice a halfpennie a pounde.

Water drunck warme — The ordinarie drinke of the common people is water which with there meate they drinke warme, houldinge it to be a soveraigne remeadie against wormes in the mawe, Other drinck they haue none, but what is distilled out of Rice which is allmost as stronge as our Aquavitæ and in culler like to Canary wine and is not Deere, yet when they haue drawne of the best and strongest, they wringe out of it a smaller and sleighter drinck, servinge the poorer sorte of people, which throughe want cannot reach to the better /

| | 30 | Wee weare furnished with 19 horse at the Emperours charge to carrie vpp our kinges presente and those that attended me to Surunga, I had a Pallankin appointed for me and a spare horse ledd by to ride when I pleased, verie well sett out, 6 men appointed to carrie my Pallankin in plaines and even grounde but where the countrie grewe hillie 10 menn were allowed me thereto / The Guardian whome kinge Ffoyne sent alonge with me did from time to time and place to place by warrant take vpp these menn and horses to serve our turnes as the Postmaisters doe heere in England, as alsoe lodginge at night accordinge to the Custome of the Countrie. I had a slave appointed to runn with a Pike before me /

| September | 6 | Thus wee travelled vntill the 6 of September, before wee gott to Surunga dailie 15 or 16 leagues of 3 miles to a league as wee guesse it. The waie for the most parte is wonderfull even and where it meeteth with mountaines passage is cutt throughe, This waye is the mayne roade of all this countrie and is for the most parte sandie and gravell, It is devided into leagues and at every leagues end

1613   The Cittie Surunga

September. 6

end, are two small hills vizt of either side of the waye one, and vppon everie one of them a faier pyne tree, trimmed rounde in fashion of an Arbor. These markes are placed vppon the waie to the ende that the harkney men, and those which lett out horses to hyre, should not make men paie more then theire due which is about iijd. a league. The roade is exceed inglie travelled, full of people, ever and anon you meete with farmes and contrie howses, with villages and often with greate Townes, with fferries over fresh rivers, and many Fotiquis which are theire Churches, situate in Groaves and most plesant places, for delight of the whole Countrie. The Priests that tend thereuppon dwellinge about the same about ffriers would fine planted themselves heere in England. When wee approched any towne wee sawe Crosses with the deade bodies of those whoe had byn crucified thereuppon. For crucifyinge is heere an ordinarie punishment for most malefactors.

Tommee neere Surunga, where the Emperors courte is wee sawe a Scaffold with the heades of divers (which had byn executed) placed thereuppon, and by it were diverse Crosses wth the dead Corpses of those which had byn executed, remayninge still vppon them, and the peeces of others, which after theire Executions, had byn hewen agayne and agayne by the triall of theire Cattans. All which caused a most vnsavorie passage to vs that to enter into Surunga, must needes passe by them.

Surunga a verie greate Cittie.

This Cittie of Surunga is full as bigge as London with all the Subvrbes. The handicraftes men wee founde dwellinge in the outward partes and skirtes of the towne because those that are of the better sorte dwell in the inward parte of the cittie, and will not be annoied with the rapping knocking and other disturbance that Artificers cannot be without. Assoone as wee were setled in our lodginge in Surunga, I sent Mr Adams to the courte to lett the Secretarie vnderstand of my cominge and desire of as speedie dispatch as might be. Worde was returned that I was welcome, that I should rest me, and within a daie or twoo I should haue accesse to the Emperour.

7

Was spent in fittinge vpp of the Presents, and providinge little tables of slitt deale of that countrie (which smelleth verie sweete) to carrie them vppon according to the Custome.

8

I was carried in my Pallakin to the Castell of Surungo (where the Emperour keepeth his Courte) and was attended with my Marchaunts and others carrying the Presents before me. Beinge entred the Castell I passed three drawe bridges everie of which had a Corps of guarde and cominge vpp a verie faier paier of staires of stone, I was mett by two grave comelie men the one of them Codski dona the Emperors Secretarie, the other

1613   Surunga.

September 8   other Fungo dono the Admirall, whoe ledd mee into a faier roome,
matted where wee sate downe crosse legged vppon the matts. Anon
after they ledd me betwixt them into the Chamber of Presence where
was the Emperours Chaier of State, to which they wished mee to doe
reverence. It was of Cloth of Gould, about 5 foote heigh verie netchlie
sett forth for back and sides, but had noe Canapie over heade. Then they
returned back againe to the place, where before they did sitt, where
havinge staied about one quarter of an hower worde was brought,
that the Emperour was come forth. Then they rose vpp and ledd me
betwixt them vnto the dore of the roome, where the Emperour was,
makinge signes to me that I should enter in there, but durst not looke
in them selues. The Presents sent from our kinge to the Emperour
as alsoe those (with according to the custome of the countrie) I gave
vnto the Emperour as from my selfe, were placed in the saide roome, &
vppon the Matts verie orderlie before the Emperour came into it.
Cominge to the Emperour accordinge to our English complemente,
I delivered our kinges letter vnto his Maiestie, whoe tooke it in his handes
and putt it vpp towardes his forehead, and commaunded his Interpreto[r]
whoe sate a good distance from him behinde, to will Mr Adams to tell
me, that I was wellcome from a wearisome iourney, that I should take
my rest for a daie or two, and then his answer should be readie for our
kinge. Soe takinge my leave of the Emperour and cominge to the
Dore, where I had left the Secretarie and Admirall, I founde them
there readie to conduct me to the staiers head, where formerlie they mett
mee, where I tooke my Pallankin, and with my Attendaunts, returned to
my lodginge.

The Present he caused to be set apart and sent it to my lodginge in the eueninge, for beinge Secretary he might receaue no guift.

9   I went to deliver the Secretarie his Present, which in noe wise hee would
receaue, but hartilie thancked mee, sayinge that the Emperour had
commaunded the contrarie. And that it went as much as his life, yf
hee should take anie guift. But hee tooke 5 poundes of Aloes socotrina
to vse for his health. I delivered the Articles of Priviledge this daie
to Codske dona, beinge in number 14, hee requested to haue them
abreviated and made as shorte as might be, for that the people of Japan
affect brevitie.

10   The Articles soe abridged, were sent by Mr Adams to the Secretarie,
whoe shewed them to the Emperour and hee approved thereof, denyinge
one onlie, which was that whereas the Chineses had refused to trade
with the English, that in case wee should take anie of them by force,
that our nation might haue leave and libertie to bringe them into
Japan, and there make sale of the goods soe taken. At the first motion the
Emperour answered, that seeing they denied vs trade, wee might take
them. But vppon conference with the Ledger of China, the Emperors
minde was chaunged and would not allow of that article.

The

1613   The Pilgrimage to Tencheday.

September 10   The rest went passed vnder his greate seale, which is not of waxe (as ours) but stamped like a printe, and ruller'd redd.

11   The Present appointed for the Mintmaster was deliuered him, which hee tooke thanckfullie and returned to mee two Japonian gownes of taffatie quilted with silke cotten.

12   Mr. Adams was sent to the Mintmaster, being the Emperours Marchaunt, and hauing charge of his Minte and readie Moneys, a mann of verie greate esteeme with the Emperour, and one that hath vowed that whensoever the Emperour shall die, hee will cutt out his owne Gutts and die with hym.

Mr. Adams carried vnto him the perticuler pritch of our english commodities (as before is specified).

About noone the same daie, wee departed for Edoo to the Emperors sonne, beinge furnished with horse and men as formerlie.

The comtrie betwixt Surungo and Edoo is well inhabited, wee sawe many Fotoquis or Temples as wee passed. And amongst others one Image of especiall note called Dabis, made of Copper, being hollowe within but of a verie substantiall thicknes. It was in height as wee guessed from the grounde about 21 or 22 foote, in likenes of a man keen knealinge vppon the grounde, with his buttocks sittinge vppon his heeles, his Armes of wounderfull largenes, and the whole bodie proportionable, hee is fashioned wearinge of a Gowne. This Image is much reverenced by travellers, as they passe there, some of our people went into the bodie of it, and hoopt and hallowed, which made an exceedinge greate noise. Wee founde maine Characters made vppon it by passengers, whome some of my followers imitated, and made theirs in like manner. It standeth in the mayne roade of the Pilgrimage to Tencheday, which is much frequented, for night and daie, rich and poore, are cominge and goinge to visitt Tencheday.

The discription of an Image called Dabis

Mr. Adams tould mee that hee had byn at the Fotoqui or Temple dedicated to this Tencheday, to whome they make this devout Pilgrimage, and as hee reported, there is monthlie out of the fairest virgins of the whole Comitrie, brought into that Fotoqui, and there shee sitts all alone in a rowme, neatelie kept, in a verie sober manner, and at certen times this Tencheday (which is thought to be the Divell) appeareth vnto her, and haueinge knowne her carnallie leaveth with her at his departure, certen seales, like vnto the seales of fishes. What questions shee is willed by the Bonzees or Priestes of that Fotoqui to aske, Tencheday resolves. And euerie moneth a fresh virgin is taken in, but what becomes of the ould Mr. Adams himselfe did not knowe.

Wee arived

1613.   The Cittie Edoo.

September 14.   Wee arived at Edoo, a cittie much greater then Surungo, farr
Ariued at Edoo   fairer buildinge, and made a verie glorious appearaunce vnto vs, the
                 ridge tiles, and corner tiles, with lie guilded, the postes of theire dores
                 guilded and garnished. Glasse windowes they haue none, but
                 greate windowes of boarde openinge in leaues, well sett out in ∞ ∞
                 paintinge as in Holland. There is a causey which goeth through
                 the cheefe streete of the towne, vnderneath this causey runneth a
                 river. At euerie 50 paces there is a well head fitted verie substan=
                 tiallie of free stone with Bucketts for the neighbours to fetch water
                 and for danger of fier. This streete is as broade as anie of our ∞ ∞
                 streetes in England.

            15. I gaue the kings secrettarie Sadda dona to vnderstand of my
                 ariuall, requestinge him to let the king knowe thereof.

            17. I had accesse to the kinge and deliuered him the Presents from our
                 king as also certen from my selfe, accordinge to the custome of the
                 Countrie) The kinge kept his Courte in the Castell of Edoo which
                 is much fairer and stronger then that of Surunga, hee was better
                 guarded and attended vppon then the Emperour his father.

                 Sadda dona the kings secretarie, is father to Codske dona the
                 Emperours secretarie, whose yeares affoarding better experience,
                 hee is therefore appointed to haue the gouernment and direction of
                 the younge king, whoe at our beinge there) wee esteemed to be aged
                 about 42 yeares.

                 My entertainment and accesse to the kinge heere was much like
                 to the former at Surunga with the Emperour, hee accepted verie
                 kindelie our kings letters and Presents, biddinge me welcome ∞ ∞
                 wishinge me to refresh my selfe, and his letters and Presents to our
                 king should be made readie with all speede.

            19. I deliuered Sadda-dona his Presents. This daie 32 men beinge
                 commaunded to a certen howse, for not payinge theire debts, and
                 beinge in the Stockes within the howse, the howse in the night
                 time, by rascaltie fiered, and they all burnt to death.

                 Towardes eueninge the kinge sent two varnished Armours for a
                 Present to our kinge, Hee sent likewise a Tatch, or long sworde,
                 which none maie weare there, but souldiers of the best ranck, and
                 a Waggadashe for a present to my selfe.

                 From Edoo to the furthermost parte of Japan, it is esteemed 22.
                 daies Journey by horse, little more or lesse.

            21. Wee parted by boate from Edoo to Oringgaw, a towne vppon the
                 seaside, from whence wee ariued at Surunga the 29 daie, and there
                 remayned for the Emperours letters, and Presents to our king.

                                                                        The. 8.

1613.
October 8.

The Emperours letter.

I receaved the Emperours letters directed to our Soveraigne Lord James kinge of Greate Britaine, the true coppie whereof is as followeth. Vizt

To the king of greate Britaine.

Your Maiesties kinde letter sent vnto me by your servant Captaine John Saris (whoe is the first that I haue knowne to ariue in anie parte of my Dominions) I hartelie imbrace, being not a little gladd to vnderstand of your greate wisdom and power as hauing three plentifull and mightie kingdomes vnder your powerfull commaunde. I acknowledge yor Maiesties greate bountie in sending me soe vndeserved a Present, of many rare thinges such as my Land affoordeth not, Neither haue I ever before seene. Which I receaue not as from a stranger, but as from your maiestie whome I esteeme as my self. Desiring the continuance of ffriendshipp with your Highnes. And that it maie stand with your good liking to send your subiects to anie parte or Porte of my Dominions, where they shalbe most hartlely welcome, applauding much theire worthines in thadmirable knowledge of Nauigation, having with much facilitie discovered a Countrie soe remott, being no whitt amazed with the distance of soe mightie a Gulfe, nor greatenes of such infinite Clowdes and Stormes, from prosecuting honorable enterprizes, of Discoveries and merchandizing. Wherein they shall finde me to further them according to theire desires. I returne vnto your Maiestie a small token of my love (by your said subiect) desiringe you to accept thereof, as from him that much reioiceth in your friendshipp. And whereas your maiesties subiects haue desired certen priviledges for trade and setling of a Factorie in my Dominions, I haue not onelie graunted what they demaunded, but haue confirmed the same vnto them vnder my Broade Seale, for better establishing thereof. Ffrom my Castell in Surunga, this 4 daie of the 9th moneth in the 18 yeare of our Dary, according to our Computation. Resting your Mats ffreinde

The highest Commaunder in this kingdome of Japan.

Subscribed. Minna Monttono. yei. ye. yeas.

Jalsoe

1613
October. 8

Priuiledges for trade in Iapan

I alsoe receaved the said Priviledges for trade in Iapan, the translation whereof, as neere to the originall, as maye be, followeth   viz̄

Priuiledges graunted

by Ogosho-sama, Emperour of Japan, vnto the Right wor:ll S:r Thomas Smyth knight, Governour, and others the honorable and wor:ll Aduenturers to the East Indies.

1. **Inprimis**, wee giue free licence to the subiects of the king of greate Britaine viz:t Sir Thomas Smith Governo:r and Companie of the East Indian merchaunts and Adventurers, forever safelie to come into anie of our Portes of our Empire of Japan with their shipps and marchaundizes without anie hindraunce to them or theire Goods And to abide, buy, sell, and barter according to theire owne manner with all nations, To tarrie heere as long as they think good, and to depart at theire pleasures/

2. **Item** wee graunt vnto them freedome of Custome for all such marchaundizes as either nowe they haue brought or heereafter shall bring into our kingdomes, or shall from hence transport to anie forraigne parte And wee authorize those Shipps that heereafter shall ariue and come from England to proceede to present sale of theire Commodities without further cominge or sending vp to our Courte/

3. **Item** if anie of theire shipps shall happen to be in danger of Shippwrack wee will our subiects not onelie to assist them, but y:t such parte of shipp and goods as shalbe saved, be returned to theire Captaine, or Cape merchaunt or theire Assignes And that they shall or may build one howse or more for themselues in anie parte of our Empire where they shall think fittest, And at theire departure to make sale thereof at theire pleasure/

4. **Item** if anie of y:e English merchants or other shall departe this life within our Dominions, the goods of the deceased shall remaine at the dispose of the Cape marchant And that all offences committed by them shalbe punished by the said Capt merchaunt according to his discretion, And our lawes to take not hould of theire Persons or Goods

Item

1613.
October

Oringaw a good harbour/

5. **Item** wee will that our subiects trading with them for any of theire commodities, paie them for the same according to agreement without delaie, or returne of theire wares againe vnto them/

6. **Item** for such Commodities as they haue nowe brought, or shall heereafter bring fitting for our service and proper vse, wee will that noe arrest be made thereof, but that the price be made with the Cape marchaunt according as they maie sell to others, and present payment vppon the deliverie of the Goods/

7. **Item** yf in discoverie of other Countries for trade and returne of theire shippes they shall neede menn or victualls, wee will that yet our subiects furnish them for theire money as theire neede shall require/

The discoverie of the Yeadzo to the Northward

8. **And** that without other Passport, they shall and maie sett out vppon the discoverie of Yeadzo, or anie other parte in or about our Empire/

From our Castell in Surunga this first daie of the nynth moneth And in the 18 yeare of our Dary according to our computation/

Sealed with our broade Seale &c/

Minna. Mottono. yei. ye yeas./

These Priviledges were written in the China character and language, and were sealed with a broade seale, which is not of way but a stampe or print vppon paper as aforesaid/

Oringgaw the best hauen for vs/

Nota that Oringgaw is a verie good harbor for shippinge where shippes maie ride as safelie, as in the river of Thames before London And the passage thereto by sea verie safe and good, soe that it wilbe much better for our shippes to saile thether, then to Firando, in respect that Oringgaw is vppon the maine Island, and is distant from Edoo (the cheef cittie) but 14 or 15 leagues/ The place is not soe well replenished with victuall and fflesh meate as Firando is, which want onelie excepted, Oringgaw is for all other matters to be preferred before Firando/

A Spanish Embassadour from the Philippinas/

At my returne to Surungo I founde a Spanish Embassadour arived there from the Philippinas who onelie had sight of the Emperour and delivered him his Presents which were certen China Damasks and 5 ffarrels of sweete wine of Europe, After the first time hee could not obtaine accesse to the Emperour/ His Embassage was

1613   A Proclamation against Christians.

October. 8   was, That such Portingalles and Spaniardes as were within
his Dominions, not aucthorized by the kinge of Spayne might be
delivered vpp vnto him to carrie awaie to the Philipinas, which
the Emperour denied to doe, saying that his countrie was a free
Countrie and none should be forced out of it, but if the Embassador
could perswade anie to goe, they should not be staied/

This cominge of the Spanish Embassador for men was caused by
the greate want of menn they had to defend the Molucca Islandes,
from the Dutch, whoe then made greatt preparation for the
absolute Conquest thereof./

After that the Embassador had attended for the Emperor's aunswer,
the time limited by his Commission seeing it came not he departed
discontented/ But being at the sea side, there was an aunswer returned vnto him to tarrie, with a slender Present, viz: fyve
Japan gownes, and two Cattanes or swordes/

9   Wee departed from Surunga./

Nota. That at Edoo, about a moneth before my cominge thether,
the Emperour being displeased with the Christians made proclamation that they should forthwith remove and carrie awaie all theire
Churches to Langasaque, a towne situate on the sea side, and distant
from Firando about 8 leagues, And that noe Christian church
should stand or Masse be singe within tenn leagues of his Courte,
vppon paine of death. A while after certen of the naturalls, being
27 in number (menn of good fashion) were assembled together, in
an hospitall appointed by the Christians for Leapers, and there had
a Masse, whereof the Emperour being informed, commaunded them
to be shutt vpp in a howse for one night, and that the next daie they
should suffer death. The same eveninge another man for debt was
clapt vpp in the same howse, being a heathen at his cominge in, and
ignorant of Christ and his religion./ But, which is wonderfull,
the next morninge, when the officer called at the Dore for those which
were christians to come forth and goe to execution, And those which
were not and did renounce the same to staie behinde, This mann in
that nightes space was soe instructed by the other, that resolutelie
hee came out with the rest, and was crucified with them/.

In our passage towardes Meaco from Surunga we had for the
most parte much rayne whereby the waters did soe rise, soe that wee
were informed to staie by the waie, soe that it was the 16 of October
before wee gott thether/

The discription of   Meaco is the greatest cittie of Japan consisting most vpon marchan-
Meaco   =dizinge, The cheefe Fotoqui or temple of the whole countrie is there,
                                                                            beinge

A Proclamation against the Chris-tians

1613
October 19 — The cittie Meaco

being built of ffreestone and is as longe as the west end of St
Paules in London, from the Quier being as hyght arched and
borne vppon pillers as that is, where verie manie Bonzees doe
attend for theire maintenaunce (as the Priestes amongst the
Papistes) There is an Alter whereuppon they doe offer rice and
small money called Cundrins (whereof 20 make one shillinge —
English) which is imployed for the vse of the Bonzees. Neere vnto
this Alter, there is an Idoll by the nationalles called Mannada
made of Copper much resembling that of Dabis, formerlie spoken
of, but is much higher, for it reacheth vpp to the verie Arch.
This Fotoqui was begunn to be built by Taico Sama in his
life tyme and since his sonne hath proceeded to the finishinge
thereof which was newelie made an end of when wee were there.
Within the inclosure of the walles of this Fotoqui, there are
buried (by the reporte of the inhabitants) the Eares and Noses
of 3000 Coreans which were massacred at one tyme vppon
theire Grave There is a Mount raised with a Pyramis on the
topp thereof, which mount is greene and verie neatelie kept.

The horse that Tiqua Sama last rode vppon, is kept neere vnto
this Fotoqui, having never byn ridden sine, his hoofes beinge
extraordinarilie growne with his age and still standinge there.

The Fotoqui standeth vppon the topp of an highe hill, and on
eitherside as yee mount vpp to it, hath 50 pillers of ffreestone,
distant ten pacts one from the other And on everie piller a
Lanthorne wherein everie night lighted are maintained of
Lampoyle.

The newe Testament in the Japan Language

In this cittie of Meaco, the Portingall Jesuittes haue a verie
statelie Colledge wherein likewise are diverse Jesuitts naturall
Japonians which preach And haue the Newe Testament printed
in the Japan Language. In this Colledge are manie Japonian
Children trained vpp, and instructed in the rudiments of Christian
religion accordinge to the Romish Church. There are not lesse
then ffyve or 6000 Japonians in this Cittie Meaco, professing
Christ.

Besides the Fotoqui before discribed, there are manie other
Fotoquis in this cittie. The tradesmen and Artificers are
distributed by themselues everie occupation and trade in theire
severall streetes, and not mingled togither as heere with vs.

At Meaco, wee staied, expecting the Emperors Present,
which at length was delivered vnto me out of the Castell
beinge 10 Beobs or large Pictures to hange a chamber w[i]t[h]

20
Wee

1613.   Our returne to Firando.

October 20 Wee departed from Meaco, and came the same
           night to Fushami.

        21 About noone wee arived at Ozacca, heere wee founde the
Osaca   people verie rude, following vs crying Tosin Tosin, that
           is Chinaes, Chinaes, others called vs Core, Core, and
           flinging stones at vs, the gravest people off the towne not
           once reprovinge them for it, but rather animatinge off
           them and setting them on/
           Heere wee founde the Gallie readie, which had attended for
           mee, ever since my landinge, at the charge off the kinge off
           Firando/

        24 At night wee all imbarked for Firando/

Novemb⁵ 6 Wee arived at Firando, and were kindelie bidd welcome
           by kinge Foyne/ All this while our people could little the
           custome off the countrie beinge, that without expres
           permission from the Emperour, noe stranger maie offer
           Goodes to sale/ Besides, our cheefest commoditie intended
           for those partes beinge broadecloth, which according to
           former intelligence had lattlie bene soulde there at 40 Royalls
           off 8. which is 8 poundesterlinge, the Royall rated at iiij ͬ
           the Matt, which is two yardes as aforsaide, the nation allso
           went nowe more backwarde to buy then before, because they
           sawe, that wee our selues went not forwarder, in weareinge
           the thinge which wee recommended vnto them/ For said
           they, you commend your cloth vnto vs, but you yo⁴ selues
           weare least thereof, the better sort of you wearinge silken
           Garementes, the meaner ffustians, &c. Wherefore hopinge
           that good counsell maye (thought late) come to some good
           purpose, I wish, that our nation, would be more forward to
           vse and spend this naturall commoditie of our owne
           Cuntrie, soe shall wee the better incouragie and allure others
           to the entertainement and expence thereoff/

        26 I assembled my marchandizinge counsell, which, vppon these
           considerations viz⁺ the incouragement that wee had receaved
           in the Moluccas by privat intelligence, the Dutch ffactorie
           allreadie planted heere, in Firando, the large priviledges nowe
           obtained of the Emperour of Japan, the rexten advice of the
                                                              English/

1613 — Our Factorie left in Japan.

November 26.

English ffactories setled in Siam, and Patane, The commodities restinge vnsould vppon our handes &c. appointed for these partes, And the hoped for proffitt, which further experience maie produce, It was resolved that a ffactorie should be left heere, viz: Eight English, 3 Japan Jurebassaes, or interpreters and two servauntes, whoe were appointed against the comminge of the next shipps to searth and discover the Coast off Corea, Tushmay, and other partes of Japan, and countries thereunto adioyninge, to see what good might be donne in anie of them.

An English factory planted in Japan.

December 5.

Mr Richard Cocke Captaine and Cape marchaunt of the English ffactorie setled at Firrando in Japan tooke his leave of vs, aboarde the Cloave with his Companie being 8 English and fyve others, after theire departure our Companie was mustred aboarde findinge

46	English	
05	Swartes	
15	Japanners		In all — 69.
03	Passengers	

Havinge lost since our arrivall heere 3 English two by sicknes, one slayne and 1 which rann awaye to the Portugalls and Spaniardes whilest I was at the Emperours Courte. The winde N.Ly. a stiff gale wee sett saile from the place where wee ridd our course S. by W. ½ a pointe W. Latt. 33d 14 minutes.

Wee returne home from Japan.

Nota that by exact observation on the shoare wee founde this Islande of Firrando, to stand in the Latt. 33d. 30 minutes : Var: 2d. 50m. Ely.

Variation at Firrando 2d 50 minuts Ely.

It was resolved to keepe alongest the Coast of China directlie to Bantam and soe wee brought aboarde our Starr boarde tack and steered awaie S.W. edginge over for China, the winde at N.N.E. a stiff gale and faire weather.

wee sailed alongst the coast of China.

6. Latt. 31d. 39m. way S by W 40 leagues.

7. It blewe verie much winde a storme, at N.W. wee steered S.S.W. no observation, heere wee felt the greate currant which shooteth out betweene the Island Corea and the mayne of China which made a verie greate Sea. Way S.S.W. ½ pointe westerlie. 25 leagues.

A greate current shootinge betweene Corea and the mayne of China.

8

1613.   Our returne from Iapan.

December .. 8   Lattitude 29° 41ᵐ wais S:W 26 leagues winde N:W a verie
                stiff gale wee steered W S:W to make Cape Sumbor uppon the Coast
Sumbor   of China the sea verie much growne soe much winde that it blowe
                our Mayne course out of the bolt ropes

         9   Lattitude 28° 23 m way S:W ¾ westerlie 22 ⅔ leagues wee sounded
                and had 49 and 45 fathom oaz the weather steered and the winde
                came to the N: but wee could see noe land

         11   Noe observation way W.S.W 35 leagues verie greene water wee
                kept our leade and had 49 43 35 37 30 ffathom: noe sight of
                land yet verie steere winde N and N.W by N

         12   Before daie wee sounded and had 35 fathom oaz winde N and N.W
                by N a stiff gale and in the morninge esteeminge our selues neere the
300 sailes of   coast of China wee had sight of at least 300 saile of Iunckes of 20
smale fishermen 30 and upwardes tunnes apeere whereof two came to the windeward
                close by us, but perceaving them to be fishermen, wee lett them passe
                using all the faier meanes wee could to gett some of them aboarde but
                could not prevaile. Whereforte wee stoode on our course W by S and
                presentlie discried the land being two Islandes called the Islandes of
                Fishers bearing W by N ½ pointe northerly some 4 leagues of
Lattitude 25.59 Lattitude at noone 25° 59 minutes way S W by W 50 leagues
                Depth 20 and 26 ffathom

                Soone after the winde came to N.E wee brought our Larboard
                tack aboarde and steered alongest the land S.S.E verie much
A Rocke   winde: About 7 at night wee came faier by a rock which by
                Gods mercie wee discried by moone light and last night in our course
                supposinge to haue runne from noone to this time 12 leagues wee
                weere within twice our shipps length of the rock depth 30 fathom
                Then wee haled of S: one watch to give the land a berth and after
                mid night steered S:W the winde at N.E verie much winde and
                continuallie followinge us as the land trents

         13   Lattitude 24° 35ᵐ Var: 01 30ᵐ Ely way S:W 54 leagues winde at
Variation 01°   N.E faier weather wee steered S:W keepinge faier by the Islands
30. minutes Ely lying alongest the mayne of China some 5 leagues of much winde

         14   In the morninge little winde having this night past had 12 and 14
                ffathomes then stoode of into deepe water Lattitude at noone 22
Lattitude 22°   10 minutes way S:W by S ¼ W ly 42 leagues winde at E.N.E
10. m   and at 8 at night wee had 15 13 ffathomes at 9 a clock 16 27 21
                and 25 sandy grounde

         15   Morning wee came amongest manye fisher boates but had soe much
Manie fisher   winde as that wee could not speake with them They made signes
boates   to us to keepe upp to the Westward (as wee thought) Our soundings
Lattitude 21 40ᵐ the last night to this present was 20 24 25 20 ffathom 3 leagues
                                                                of the

1613   The Coast of China

December — 14   of the land Lattitude at noone 21° 40 minutes, way W. S. W. ¼ S'ly, 52 leagues, The winde at N. N. E. a stiffe gale wee steered in W. N. W. N'ly to make the land and about two howers after had sight of it, But by reckoninge should not have beene neere it by 56 leagues, Soe that the distance from Firando hether is lesso by 56 leagues.

Nota, that the Ilandes which lye alongest the coast of China lye more S'ly, then in the platte, for about 3 in the afternoone wee steered by an Island called Lancha, about 2 leagues of, wee steered S. W. alongest the land, esteeminge to have rune since our Noone 5 leagues W. N. W.

16   At noone noe observation wait 40 leagues S. W by S. ¼ W'ly, winde at E. with drislinge rayne.

Latt. 18° 19 minuts
var: 50 minuts
Westerly

17   Lattitude 18° 19 minutes, course S. W by S. ¼ W'ly 47 leagues, — winde at E. Variation 50m W'ly S. W by S. Wee sounded, but had noe grounde.

18   Lattitude 15° 43 minutes course S. W. by S. 60 leagues winde at E. a stiff gale and at satt night wee had sight of land, beinge an Island called *Pulo Cotan* bearing W. S. W about 5 leagues of, wee steeringe S. W. This Island is highe land and lieth about 20 leagues (by reporte) from the shoale called *Plaxel*, to the westward of it, Wee sounded about 8 of the clock but had noe grounde.

Pulo Cotan

Plaxel

Cambora

19   Morninge the mayne of Cambora was on our starreboarde side about two leagues of, wee steered alongest S. by E. E'ly, keepinge the mayne in sight. Lattitude at noone 13° 31 minutes waye S. by W. 44 leagues, yet steered alongest S. S. W. makinge an attompt to be thwart the A Varella, keeping about 2 leagues of the shoare, wee sounded, but had noe grounde at 50 ffathom.

A Varella

Cambora is not so farr esterly as it is sett in our Platte

Nota that this land of Cambora lieth more E'ly in our platte, then it should, for wee finde S. S. W. to goe alongest the land a faire berth of, Soe that the land heere lieth S. S. W. and N. N. E. & havinge diverse rockes like Ilandes, some one league some 1½ league of the mayne, but otherwise noe danger that wee could see.

Nota also that heere wee fonnd the windes trade alongest the shoare, ffor from Firando hether wee did not large, findinge the winde to followe us as the land trents.

20   Lattitude 10° 53 minutes course S. by W. 54 leagues winde at N. a stiff gale alongest the shoare, And 3 glasses after wee had observed wee had sight of a small Island which wee made to be the Island at the end of the shoale called *Pulo Citi*, And at 5
                                                                     glasses

Pulo Citi or Pulo Cecir

1613.   The Coast of China.

December 20 Glasses runing wee sounded and 11 ffathom fine sand 2 leagues
             of the shoare, wee steered alongest S.W. to bring the point of the
             shoale called Pulo Citi a sterne: then wee sounded about two glasses
             after, and had 15 ffathom/
             Nota, that wee founde Jan Huyghen van Linschotens booke
             verie true: for thereby wee directed our selues euen from our ∞ ∞
             setting forth from Firando/

        21   Lattitude 9°.43ᵐ course S.W. ¼ W.ly. 34 leagues. winde at E. N. E.
             a continuall stiff gale till noone, then calme and founde that wee
             weare in a tide girt, our depth all the last night to this noone
             was 10. 16. 17. 18. 21. 21. 19. 20. 20. 19. 18. ffathom good grounde,
             but had not sight of land/

Pulo Condor 22 In the morning wee had sight of land being an Island called Pulo
Latt: 8°.20.m   Condor bearing of vs about 5 leagues off. wee steered S.W. the wind
                at N.E. Lattitude at noone 8 degrees 20 minutes way S.W. by W.
                40 leagues ⅔ Depth 18. 19. 22. 21. 21. 22. and 21 ffathom wee steered
                S.S.W. for the land called the 7 pointes/

        23   No obseruing/. way S.W. by S. ¼ S.ly. 51 leagues. depth 20. 22. 24.
             and at noone 27 ffathom/

        24   way S.W. ½ pointe westerlie 33 ½ leagues winde at N.W. by N.
             Depth 37. 39. 43. 40. and at noone 35 ffathom. Oaz grounds/

Latt 2°.38.m 25 Lattitude 2°. 38.m course S. by E. ¼ E.ly 22 ⅓ leagues the winde at
                 N.W. and E by N: Depth 34. 32. 30. 34. 34. 34. 35/ And about
                 4. of the clock in the morninge, wee made the land being an Island
Pulo Timon   called Pulo Timon distant from vs some 5 leagues and at 6 in
                 the morning the Nethermost parte bearing S.W. W.ly. and the S.
                 parte S.S.W. ¼ a point W.ly. wee had sight of an other Island called
Pulo Tmga   Pulo Tmga bearing S.S.W. westerlie about 6 leagues off at noone/

        26   Lattitude 01°.18.minutes course S. E by S. 32 leagues winde at E. and
             E by N: Depth 37. 36. 37. 35. 30. and 27 ffathom/

        27   Course S. by E. 40 ⅔ league depth 27. 31. 28. 29. 28. 26. and 24. ff
             fathom at noone/

        28   way S.S.E 40 ⅔ league depth 18. 19. 16. 18. 19. 16. and at noone
             15 ffathom sandie grounde makinge accompt that China Bata e
             was about 1 ½ league of beinge lowe land, and at the S.W point,
             full of trees or bushes. At 6 glasses after noone wee sounded and
             had 20 fathom oazie grounde, steeringe alongest the lande S.S. E. the
             winde at N. N. W / Nota: that those longe Islandes on our
             Starboarde side heere and diuers small Islandes on our Larboord side
                                                                              Doe

1613   China bata.

December   **28**   Doe make the straightes of China Bata, findinge it to be trulie

The Platt of Jan Janson Mold   laide downe in the Platt or Draft made by Jan Janson Mole a Holander.

29 A little before noone wee perceaved the water to be much changed

A dangerous Shoald not farr from the entraunce of the straight of Chinabata   ahead, and therefore doubted it to be a shoale, soe narrowlie escaping a verie greate danger wee sownded and had. 11. 12. 14. 15. ffathom but within halfe a glasse had 8. and 7½ ffathom. It seemed there square and sharpe to the S.W. warde, and soe wee steered when wee had first sight thereof, not farr from the entraunce of the straights of China Bata. This shoale lieth verie dangerouslie but is trulie

Lattitude 4°. 6. m.   placed with his Depthes. Latt at noone 04d. 06 minutes, course S by W. 30 leagues, winde at N.W. and N. Depth 20. 13. 14. 24. 27. 20. 25. 20. 18. 10. 10. 10. 8. and 10. ffathoms soft sand and at 8. of the clock in the night wee came to an Ancker in 7 fathom. the weather likelie to be fowle, and our experience little or nothinge the place verie full of shoales, and before our Ancker was aGrounde wee were in 6. 6¼. 5½. 6. and then in 7. fathom soft sandie grounde, the winde at N.W. a smale gale and raynye.

30 This morninge, wee had sight of the Darling plying for Coroman

The Darling sailing for Coromandell   dell her Companie 21 English and 9 Swartes. By them wee first understoode of the death of Sir Henry Midleton, and losse of ye Trades increase &c. The wether close wee observed not, Way. S.S.W. ½ pointed W. 15 leagues Depth. 10. 13. 14. 11. 10. 9. 8. 7. 6½. 10. 10. 6½. 7. 5. 4½. 5. 5. and 4 fathom, hard sandie grounde, esteeminge this the shoales described in Moles Platt, and not that which wee made it for. This night God mercifullie delivered

A sunken ledge of Rockes   vs out of a greate danger, ffor wee passed by a sunken ledge of Rockes under all our sailes within a stones cast of the topp thereof which was onelie seene above water, and had not the noise of the breach uppon it, wakened vs wee could not have steered our selves, wee did lett fall our ancker presentlie beinge in a greate tide guirt, and had. 17. 17½ ffathom oaze ground.

The highland of Sumatra   **31** In the morninge as wee ridd the hight land of Sumatra was about 10 leagues of vs, and one Island asterne. Wee passed shoale or ledge of rockes on the starboarde side, and 3 small Islandes on our larboarde bowe, lying 3 square. Way S. ¾ Ely. 21 leagues, winde at N.W. Depth. 10. 9. 8. 7. 9. 10. 11. 12. 15. 22. ffathom, about. 8 leagues of ye highe land of Java, wee could not gett in because it fell calme.

Ianuarie   **1** Beinge calme was most spent at an Ancker.

2 Having a little winde wee sett saile, and about 8 of the clock met with

1613 — Our returne to Bantam

Ianuarie 2.

The Expedition bound for England

with the Expedition and vnderstanding that shee was bound homeward laden with Pepper, wee writt by them to our ffrindes in England.

Wee arrived in Bantam roade.

3. Wee came to an Ancker in Bantam Roade, finding (to our greate greefe) noe lading in readines, ffor which I iustlie blamed those whome I had left there to provide the same, whoe excused themselues sayinge, that they did not as yet expect me. I questioned with Keewee the cheefe marchaunt of the Chineses (being come aboarde to visitt mee) what price pepper did beare, and howe hee would sell. Hee aunswered, that it was alreadie knowne a ffarr part that I was homeward bounde, and comight of necessitie lade pepper, Whereof my marchants hauinge provided none aforehand I might be assured it would rise, hee saide, it was then at 12 R.s of 8. the 10 sackes, but hee would not vndertake to deliuer anie quantitie at that price. I offred him 12½ R.s for 10 sackes but founde him soe farre of, as that there was noe hope of dealinge at the present.

Note, that of the 10. left in the Factorie heere, for the 8.t Voiage, at o.r departure for Japan wee founde nowe but 5 liuinge at our returne hether. Betweene Firando and Bantam wee lost onelie one.

4. In the morning I went ashoare, vizited the Governour of Bantam and presented him with two faier Cattans and divers other thinges of worth.

This daie I bargained with Keewee and Lackmoyle, for 4000 sackes of Pepper at 13 R.s of 8. the ten sackes. Basse .3. p. Cent: and appointed the marchants to hasten the millinge thereof all that might be.

5. Was spent in reducinge the severall English factories in Bantam to one Governement and settling them in one howse. And order was taken that the expence of dyett should be more frugallie managed, then of late it had byn, And that the Warehowses in the Towne should be fewer in number, and better looked vnto as well it might be, the goods beeinge with more distretion orderlie stoed.

The severall English factories in Bantam reduced into one.

6. In the reweyinge of the pepper, wee receaved the daie before, wee found most of the sackes hard waight and many to want of what the kinges beame did allowe, wherefore I sent for the mayer, vsed him kindlie, and intreated him to take a little more care and paynes, to amend this fault, which hee promised to doe, Whereto the better, to incourage him I appointed the value of 5. R.s of 8. to be giuen him.

Divers gentlemenn of the countrie came to visitt me aboarde, havinge byn of my ould arquamtaunce.

8. Wee begann to lade, but it proved soe raynie, that we could take in but 500 sackes.

The President

1613   The King of Iapans letter.

Ianuarie — 15 The President and marchaunts of the Dutch factorie came to visitt me in the English howse, where I friendlie intreated promisinge to requite them with the like curtesie, assoone as oc‑ casion would permitt.

16 Being the Sabaoth daie I staied aboarde About two of the clock in the afternoone, the Towne was all on a fier wherefore our Skiff, being well mand, was presentlie sent ashoare to help the marchannts to guarde the goods. The winde was soe violent that in a moment of time, allmost the whole towne was burnt downe. The English and Dutch howses excepted, which it pleased God of his mercie to preserve.

The whole towne of Bantam burnt downe sauing the English and Halanders howses.

20. Being ashoare I procured Lackmoye and Lanching two cheese marchannts to translate the letter which the kinge of Firando in Japan had delivered mee to carrie to our king Iames. It was written in China Charecters and Language they translated it into the Malayan, which in English is as followeth viz.

To the King of Greate Britaine &c.

Most mighty king, how

acceptable your Maiesties loving letter, and bountifull present, of manie worthie thinges, sent me by your servaunt Captaine John Saris, is vnto me, I cannot sufficientlie expresse. Neither the greate happines I esteeme my self to be in, by enioying your highnes ffriendshipp, ffor which I render you many thanckes, desiring the continuance of your maiesties love and acquaintance. I am hartelie gladd of your subiects safe arivall at my small Iland, from so long a iourney, my help and furtheraunce they shall not want to the vttermost, for the effectnig of theire so worthie and laudable enterprizes off Discoverie, and Marchandizing, greately comending theire forwardnes therein, Referring theire hetherto entertainment, to the reporte of your servaunt, by whom I returne vnto your Maiestie an vnworthie Token, wishing your maty long life. From my Palace of Firando, the 6th daie of our tenth moneth.

yor mats loving ffrende, Comaunder of the Iland of Firando in Japan

Foyne Sama masam

1613 Bantam

Ianuarie

20 They could not well pronounce his name. ffor Lanching said, it was Foyne foshinsam. But Lackmoye said, as is aboute written.

22 Such howses as the former fier had spared, were nowe burnt downe, yet the English and Dutch howses, escaped againe, thanckes be vnto God.

26 Heere arived a ffleemish shipp of 1000 tunnes, from Holland called the ffflushing. At the Island Mayo, the Companie had mutenied against the Captaine and had murthered him in his Cabyne, but that it pleased God a Scottishman revealed the matter even when they were armed to come vppon the exploite, soe that they were taken betwixt the Deckes with theire weapons about them. In this shipp were divers *Divers English and Scottish Soldiers* — English and Scottish souldiers. Shee stayed not heere, but towardes Eveninge sett saile for Iaccatra.

27 I went ashoare to hasten the marchaunts, divers of o' companie beinge at this present sick. Our shipp had nowe our full lading in.

Februarie

1 The Darling, having by stormes and contrarie windes broke her Mayne yarde and sprung her mayne mast, was inforced to returne hether, ffor whose better dispose, I caused a meetinge of my marchan-dizing councell, whereby it was ordred, That in regarde the Monsoone did not permitt her to proceede to the coaste of Coromandell, her Comodities fitting for England should be souldunto vs for the 8.th vo: as they cost, and that shee should be sent with all speede to Socodamia to visitt the ffactorie there, and from thence in Aprill to goe for Patane and Siam, where visitinge these ffactories and findinge noe beneficiall employement from theire direction, Then with a convenient stock of Money (which shee had with her) and certen Cambaya goods vendible in those partes, To provide to lade the best silkes at Patane and Beniamyn at Siam, that they might procure, and soe to returne to Bantam, where the ffactorie should then determine of her further imployement, as tyme should present occasion. ffor the takinge in of these Goods, wee were forced to staie heere a little the longer. And to incourage the sailers in her, the better to proceede (being poore) I gave order that they should have 3 monethes paie apeece, and 100 R.s to the Master.

6 Vppon consideration of the greate disorder caused by the multiplicitie of ffactories of our owne nation in this place, everie one indeavoringe the proper benefitt of theire owne perticuler attompt, not heedinge the generall good of the whole Companie. Whereby all requested comodi-ties were soe raised in prise, as little good was to be donne thereuppon, To prevent this inconvenience I have order that at the arivall of the China Junckes all the Marchaunts should meete together, and consult what rates (according to the tyme and other circumstaunces) were to be

1613		The Straights of Sunda
Februarie	6	be allowed the Chineseas for theire Comodities which prized soe agreed vppon none of them to exceede without a newe consent and agreement of the rest. And yet to keepe theire attompts aparte vntill further order out of England. In the meane time, that they should settle themselves togeather in the ould howse and reduce theire Goodes to a fewe howses as they might continewinge the ould warehowse for the thiefe, and safest for the Goodes. That the charges of dietts wages &c should be every month cleared and charged to those perticuler accompts for which it had bine disbursed. That they should make away theire cloth for newe Pepper, as speedilie as they could, and to trust none without a pawne Except the king, Lackmoye, Tanyoung, and Kewee who are the principall dealers. And left them such further directions for all other matters concerninge the Trade, the government of the ment, the buildinge of a newe Godong or warehowse &c, as were thought needefull.
	13	Wee gott out of the straightes of Sunda. Nota, that in the Straightes of Sunda, the tydes sett 12 howers to the E: wardes, which is fludd, and 12 howers to the W. wardes, which is ebbe.

1614		
Maie	16	Wee came to an Ancker in the Baye of Saldania where wee founde the Concorde of London, being the first that was sett out for the home stocke. Wee founde the naturalles of this place verie tretcherous at the present making signes vnto vs of the horrible carrying away of two of theire people. They had wounded out of the Concordes menn very sore. And whilest wee were vpp in the land they did assault those that kept our Skiff, carried away our Grapnall and had spoiled those that were left to attend her, but that they tooke the water.
	19	Heere arived a Flemish shipp bounde for Bantam, the Maister Cornelis van Harte.
June		Wee remained here 23 daies and having well refreshed ourselves, tooke with vs 14 oxen, and 70 sheepe alive, besides good store of fish and beef which wee powdred there finding it to take salt well, contrary to former reportes. For 10 daies after our departure from Saldania wee had the winde at N.W. and W.N.W. but then came to S.W. soe that wee might gett our course N.W.
The beefe of Saldania taketh Salt well.		
September	27	Wee arived, (thanckes be to God) at Plimouth, where for the space of 5 or 6 weekes wee endured most tempesttous wether, and our lives more endangered, then vppon the whole voiage besides.

Since

1614
September 27

Notes for Marchandizing

Since which having had some spare tyme, I haue Collected certen Notes (in the Journall omitted) and haue thought good to place them heere, to attend the former Relation, as followeth

VI*t*

BANTAM

Bantam is a towne scituat in the Island of Iaua Maior in the latitude of 6 degrees to the South of the Equinoctiall, and hath three degrees Variation W. To this place manie nations resorte, bringinge diuers commodities, Of it self, it affoardeth little but victualls, Cotten wooll and Pepper. whereof the quantitie maie be at Harvest (which is in the moneth of October) some 30 or 32 thowsand of Sackes, each sack contayninge 49½ Catties China and each Cattie 21½ ounces English. A sack is called a Timbang. Two Timbangs make a Pecull. Three Peculls make a small Bahar, and 4½ Peculls make a greate Bahar, which is 445½ Catties.

Item there is a Coolack by which the Jauans most comonlie deale, because they are not verie perfect in the vse of the Beame. A Coolack contayneth 7¼ Catties, and 7 Coolackes make a Timbang (water measure) which is 1¼ Catties greater then the Beame. There ought to be noe difference betwixt them but that the waigher (who is allwaies a Chinesa) doth favour his countrie men and fitteth the waight to pleasure them.

In the monethes of December and Ianuarie hether come many Iunks and Prawes laden with Pepper from Cherimgin and Janby: soe that

1614. At Bantam.

September / 27

in the end of Januarie heere is att Bantam allwaies readie, &
sufficient Pepper to lade three good shyppes /

The kinge of Bantam hath noe moneie of his owne coynage
but the money vsed by the Jauans is brought out of China and is
called by them Cashes beinge made of the drosse of Leade in little
peeces rownde and thynne, with holes in the middest to string them
vppon / 1000 Cashes vppon a stringe which is called a Peecoo which
is valued diverslie higher and lower accordinge to the plentie or
scarcitie of Cashes / Herwith they passe all theire Accomptts as
followeth /   Vizt
            10 Peecoos is a Laxsaw. 10 Laxsawes is a Cattie,
            10 Catties is a Vta: and 10 Vtaes is a Bahar /

Item it is to be vnderstood that there are two sortes of stringing of
Cashes, the one called Chuchuck China. The other Chuchuck
Jaua of which the Jaua is the best / For whereas there should be
200 Cashes vppon a tack, you shall finde vppon the China tacke
but 160. or 170 / Fyve tackes should make a Peecoo, soe that you
loose 200 Cashes vppon a Peecoo or 150. which will rise to a greate
matter dealing for matter of worth / But by the lawe of the
Cuntrie they should be 1000 Cashes on a stringe, or by defalt
to give Basse, which is allowaunce /

Basse signifieth allowaunce /

Item vppon the departure of the China Junckes you may buy
34. and 35 Peecoos of Cashes for a royall of 8 which before the
next yeare (that the Junckes come againe) you maie sell for 22
and 20 Peecoos for a royall, soe that greate proffitt is to be made
thereof, but the danger of fier is greate /

The waight heere vsed for Beazars Ciuett and Gould is called a
Taile, which waieth 2¼ Royalls of 8. or 2 ounces English /
Item a Mallayo Taiel is 1½ R{s} of 8. or 1⅓ ounces English /
Item a Taiel China is 1·7⁄20 R{s} of 8. which is 1¼ ounces English
Soe that 10 Taieles China is 6 Taieles Jaua exactlie /

Item the English comodities vendible heere are as followeth / Vizt

English Iron long and thynn barres ————— 6 R{s} of 8. the Peecull
Lead in small pigge poiz 25 or 26{lb} peece ——— 5½ R{s} the Peecull
Powder fine corned corned the Barrell ————— 25 R{s} of 8.
Peeces square sanguind 6 foot long the p8 —— 10. R{s} of 8.
Peeces square damasked allover 6½ foot long — 15 R{s} the peece
Broadcloth ruller Venice redd of wch the cloth
at London the yard (which is ¾ of a yarde) & } 3 Royalls of 8
Opium Misseree which is the best the Catty ——— 8 Royalls
Amber in greate beades, one waying ½ tayle Malayo — 6 Royalls —
                                                    Currall

1614 At Bantam
September 27

The best comodity Corrall in large branches, the waight of the Mallayo taiell — 6 Royalls.

Royalls of 8 the best requested comoditie yo can carry hither; you are to knowe, that in the monethes of Februarie and March yearlie hether commeth 3 or 4 Junkes from China verie ritchlie laden with silkes both rawe and wrought, China Cashes, Porcelanes, Cotten cloth of diuers sortes and prizes — *vizt.*

Rawe silke of Lankin which is the best — 190 R[s] of 8. y[e] Peecull
Rawe silke of Canton which is courser — 80 R[s]. the Peecull
Taffita in boltes con[taining] 12 yardes the peece — 46 R[s] the Corg wth 16.20 peeces
Velvett of all cullers cont. 13 yardes the peece — 12 Royalls the peece
Damaske of all cullers cont. 12 yardes the peece — 6 R[s] the peece
White Satten 12 yardes longe the peece — 8 R[s]
Burryatos 10 yardes long the peece — 45 R[s] the Corg
Sleave silke of all cullers the best — 3 Royalls y[e] Catty
Muske the best — 22 R[s] the Catty
Sewing gould the best 15 knotts, every knot 36 threedes — 1 R[s] the 15 knotts
Velvett hangings imbrodered with gould — 18 R[s] the peece
Satten hangings imbrodered — 14 R[s] the peece
White tuftie stuffes 9 yardes long the peece — 50 R[s] the Corge
White Damask flatt 9 yardes long the peece — 4 Royalls
Suger white and verie drie — 3½ R[s] the peecull
Sugar Candie verie dry — 5 R[s] the Peecull
Porcelane or stoute basons the peece, verie broade and fyne — 2 R[s]
Callico cloth course, white and browne — 15 R[s] the Corge

Course Purcelane druggies and diuers other comodities they bring which in regard they are not for y[e] our countrie I omitt

Beniamyn verie good and white — 35 & 30 R[s] y[e] peecull
Lignum Aloes 80 R[s] — 80 R[s] the peecull
Allum (as good as our English) brought from China — 2½ R[s] the peecull

Cotten cloth of Coromandell is a principall comoditie, the sortes most vendible heere ar talled — *vizt.*
Gobars, Pintados of 4 and 5 Covetts
Fyne Tappies of Samel Thomas, Ballachios

1614   At Bantam

September

Jana Girdles otherwise called Cayn-goolong:

Callico lawnes, Booke Callicoes, and Callicoes made vpp in Rolles white.

Goobars, contayne 6 yardes the peece.

Ballachios course and fine conteyne 32 and 34 Hastas, but the finest are allwaies longest.

The fine Tappies of Samet Thomas. 6 Hastas

Booke Callicoes, and Callico lawnes (if they be not guelded or sorted) 32 Hastas.

All sortes of Mallayun cloth are generallie 8 Hastas, and are therefore called Cherra-malayo.

All sortes of Cotten clothes, which are broade and of good length are well requested heere.

Item a Hasta is half a yard longe.

The Kinges Custome and other duties payable at Bantam, are as followeth.

The Custome is called Chukey which is 8 Bagges or Sarks vppon the hundred sarks the pepper rated at 4 R^s of 8 the Sark what price soever it is bought at.

Billa-billian is. If any shipp arive in the roade laden with Cotten cloth or other comoditie, the King is first to be made acquainted therewith, and with the sortes quantitie and prices thereof before anie of the Goodes maie be landed Then hee will send his officers, and will take such sortes as him pleaseth at the half of the price or somewhat above as yee can agree. ffor if you p'rize your cloth at 20 R^s the Corge, hee will compell you to take 15 or 16 for what him liketh. But the fflemingies course hath byn to giue him 700 or 800 Royalls of 8. at a tyme for a shipps ladinge to free themselves of that dutie and troble.

But by the Custome of the countrie this duty is vppon 6000 sarkes of pepper 666 R^s of 8, yf you lade pepper, Otherwise to take soe manie thowsand sarkes of the king at ½ a Royall or ¾ of a Royall of 8. deerer the sark then the price currant in Towne. And in case you shall haue pepper provided afore hand for your lading yet you shall paie this dutie or els not be permitted to lade.

Rooba Rooba is a dutie for Anforaxye and is for 6000 sarks 500 Royalls of 8.

The Sabanders dutie is vppon 6000 sarkes 250 Royalls of 8.

The

1614
September

At Iortan &c:

The Ierotoolis (or waights belonging to the Custome house) theire dutie is one Royall vppon the 100 sackes wch whith amounteth to in Royalls — 57 3/5 Royalls of 8 vpon the hundred sackes of pepper

Nota. The Iaua Alphabet conteyneth 20 letters
The Mallayan Alphabet conteyneth — 24 letters

Iortan

Iortan is to the Eastwards of
Jaccatra and is called Serebaya it affoordeth of it self greate store of vittualls and greate store of Cotten wooll and spun yarne, hether cometh manie Iunckes from Iamby with pepper alsoe & small Prawes of this towne fett some fewe of Mace and Nutmeggs from Banda hether

Iamby

Maccasser

Maccassar a towne vpon Celebes,
affoardeth greate store of Beazar stones which are to be had at reasonable rates, alsoe Rice and other vittualls greate plentie, & Heere are Iunckes, which trade to Banda for Mace and Nutmeggs.

Maccasar a towne vppon Celebes.

Balij

Balij is an Island to the Eastwards,
of Balii Iaua Maior standing in 8½ degrees to the S° of the Equinoctiall, it hath of it self greate store of Rice, Cotten yarne, Flauid and course white cloth, which is well requested at Bantam. The comodities heere vendible are, the smallest sorte of Beades, blewe and white, Iron, and course Porclane.

Timor

1614 At Timor &c.
September.

Timor.

Timor is an Island, lying to the Eastward of Bali in Latitude 10° 40 minutes, to the S° of the Equinoctiall, it affoardeth greate store of Chin danna by us called white saunders, the greatest loggs are accompted best, It is worth at Bantam 20 R° of 8 the Peecull at the comming of the Junckes away, m greate Cakes which vs is at Bantam worth 18. 19. 20. 30 Royalls of 8 the Picull as the time serves. Be carefull in choice thereof, and breake the Cakes, for they use & much deceipt therein. The comodities vendible are Chopping knives, small Bugles, Parrelaut cullored Taffaties but noe blacke, China frying pans, China bells and peeces of silver beaten flatt and thyn as a wafer of the breadth of a hand; greate proffitt is to be made of this trade, for the Chineses have given to our menn which did adventure with them thither, fower for one.

Greate profit to be made at Timor

Banda.

Banda lieth in latitude 5. degrees to the S° of the Equinoctiall, it affoardeth greate store of Mace and Nutmeggs, with oile of both sortes, They have harvest heere thrice in the yeare viz.t in the monethes of July, October and February But the gathering in Julie is the greatest, which is called the Monson Arepooti. A small Bahar with the Bandaneses, is 10. Catties of Mace and 100. Catties of Nutmeggs. The greatt Bahar is 100. Catties of Mace and 1000. Catties of Nuttmeggs. A Cattie heere is 5 poundes 13 ½ ounces English. The prize variable as the yeare proves. The comodities heere requested are Cotten cloth of Choromandell, Cheremallay viz.t Sarassas, Pintadoes of 5 Covetts, fine Ballachios, black Girdles Chellits, white callicoes broade clothes, stamnetts, Gould coined viz.t Rose nobles of England and the Lowe Countries, Royalls of 8. You shall have that heere for 70 R.s in gould, which in silver money would cost you 90. R.s China basons fine large and without brymes, Damaskes of divers cullers Taffities, velvetts, China contores or Boxes gilded Gould chaynes, plate, cupps guilded, head peeces bright, Damasked peeces for shott but not manie, sword blades broade and backt to the pointe Cambaya cloth, Calicoes black and redd, Calico lawnes and Rice is alsoe a good comoditie there.

Siam

1614.
September.

At Siam &c:

Siam

Siam lieth in the lattitude of 14 ½ d.
to the N. of the Equinoctiall. It yeeldeth greate store of very
good Beniamin and manie rich stones which are brought thither
from Pegu. The waight of the Taiel heere is 2 ¼ R^s of 8. Heere is
much Silver in Bullion brought from Japan, but Royalls of 8. are
better requested. For 2 ¼ Royalls in coyne will yeeld 2 ½ in Bullion.
Comodities vendible heere are Broadecloth, stammett, Iron, and
faier looking glasses. All manner of China comodities are cheaper
heere then at Bantam.
The Guzzerat Junckes come to Siam in the monethes of June,
and Julie and touch first at the Maldiues, and then at
Tanasseri, from whence they maie goe overland to Siam in
twentie daies.
Att Tanasseri there is allwaies 5 ½ and 6. ffathom water.

Borneo

Borneo lieth in lattitude 3 degrees
to the S. of the Equinoxiall. It affoordeth greate store of
gould, Bezarstones, wax, Rotanes, or small canes, Cayou Lacca,
and Sanguis Draconis.
At Beniermassen a towne scituate on this Iland is the principall trade. Comodities there vendible are Cotten cloth of
Choromandell, of all sortes, China silkes, Damasks, taffaties,
velvette, All cullers except blacke, Broadecloth stammett, and
Royalls of 8. Bezarstones are here bought by the Taiel which
waieth 1 ½ Royalls of 8. which is 1 ⅓ ounces English, and will
cost 5 or 6 Roialls the Taiel.

Socadanna

Socadanna is a Towne scituated on
Borneo in the Lattitude of 1 ½ d: to the S. of the Equinoxiall,
and is N.E. from Bantam 160 leagues. In the entraunce of the
harbo^r is 5 fathom at lowe water 3 fathom. A ffalcon shott
of the shoare, oozey grounde.

1614   At Socodanna.
September

The best Diamonds are taken at Landack Sambas & Dian and brought to Socadanna.

This place is greate trade in Junckes and Prawes, It yeeldeth greate store of Diamonds being esteemed the best in the world, and plentie at all times, but especiallie in the monethes of Januarie, Aprill, Julie and October, but the greatest quantitie in Januarie and Aprill, At which times they are brought downe the river called Laue by ye Prawes. They gett them by Dyving, as divers doe Pearle. The reason whie greater quantities are gott at one tune then at another is, ffor that in Julie and October, heere falleth soe much rayne that it riseth 9 fathom which runneth such a current that they can hardlie dive, and in the other monethes there is but 4 or 4½ fathomes which is held the best depth for theire diving.

Comodities heere requested are Mallayan Intados, verie fine Sarasses, Goobarrs, Polmgs, Chera Java, Callico lawnes, & China silkes, light roulers, sewing gould, sleave silke, Broadecloth, Stammett, all sortes of small bugles, and bugles which are made in Bantam, of rouler blew, and in fashion like a tunn of the bignes of a beane, and doe cost at Bantam 400 Royall of 8, and will yeeld at Socadanna a Mass for the 100. the Mass being ¾ of a Royall of 8.

China Cashes, Royalls of 8, But cheifelie gould, without wch you can doe little; ffor you shall have a stone for the value of one Royall of 8 in gould which you shall not have for 1½ R, and 1¾ of a Royall of 8 in silver.

Being bound for this place, ye best course is to goe first to Beniermassen where you mau barter the aforesaid commodities for gould, which you shall have for 3 Catties of Cashes the Mallaian Taiel which is 9 Rs of 8. And bringing it to Socadanna you shall put your gould of for Diamonds at 4 Catties cashes the Taiel which is 1⅞ Ro of 8 in waight, soo that you shall gayne ¾ of a Royall of 8 vppon a Taiel but you must reckon your cheefe proffitt to be vppon the Diamonds

There are Diamants of fower waters / Viz.

1.	Warna Ambon
2.	Warna Lowd
3.	Warna Sackar
4.	Warna Bessi

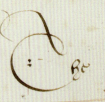

1614
September

China

The first is white, The second is Greene, the thirde yellowe, the last neither greene nor yellowe, but betweene both / The white water is the best. Their waight is called Sa-mas / Sa-coopang, Sa-boosuck, Sa-pead / A Mass is 4 Coopanges, one Coopang is 2 Boosucks, and one Boosuck is 1½ pead /

There is also a Pahaw which is 4 Mass and 16 Mass is 1 Taiel. By this waight they doe not onelie waigh Diamonds but goulds also / A Mangelle is 5 leeb, which is a Carrect good waight /

Item one Coopang is 21 leeb or 4 Carrects good waight /

One pounde Pead is 5¼ leeb or one Carrect good waight

Item 10 lees is one Saga China waight which is two Carrects good waight /

China

China is a most plesant, ritch and populous countrie, which the Naturalles well knowing, will not permitt any other nation vnder couller of trade, or otherwise to come into it, much lesse to remayne and inhabite amongs them /

It is deuided into 15 Prouinces, each Prouince having tenn greate Townes belonging to it. The names of the Prouinces (as they were delivered vnto me by a naturall Chinesa, dwelling at Bantam) are from the Northermost to the sea coast as followeth /

1	Ducking	9	Hunnam
2	Santong	10	Quichu
3	Lanking	11	Sooswan
4	Chetian	12	Sansaie
5	Cansaie	13	Outong
6	Hochian	14	Samsaie
7	Cantong	15	Chanchu
8	Quansiee		

1614.
September.

China.

The king keepeth his courte at Pucking, which province is neere adioyninge vppon Tartaria, being inclosed on that side with a greate walle, soe that the Tartars cannot offend them. The king keepeth in paie continuallie 2. Vtaes of souldiers.

A Vta is a million. vizt. 1000000. None are suffred to weare weapons but souldiers. They make Captaines of 10. of 100. and of 1000. and are knowne by the severall fashions of theire garments what companie they commaund.

If anie man take the profession of a souldier vppon him, his issue must evermore continue the same. They trayne and muster everie thirde daie.

And have theire paie everie 30. daie in silver which is cutt into peeces according to the value they are to receave, soe that everie souldier hath his beame and sheeres fitted for that purpose.

Learning is greatelie esteemed amongest them.

Noeman is admitted to take the name and title of a Lungaua vppon him (which is a Judge or otherwise imploied about Justice) but hee is first publiquelie examined by the learned of the land to see whether hee be sufficient. Divers dispute one against the other and the best deserveth carrieth it awaie, though the others be of never soe high discent, and hee never soe base of parentage. Theire disputation is in theire mother tongue, for they give not themselves to the studie of anie forraigne language. This vpright course soe strictlie observed for the openinge of the gate leading to preferment, causeth the people rather to be verie industrious to attaine vnto perfection and soe to deserve, then to hunt after money, to slubber theire insufficientcie and soe plaie the knaves or fooles when they have obtained the place. To this end the most of theire children are carefullie trained vpp to learninge.

They have publique places appointed for triall of mens sufficient=
cies in artes and exercises. vizt. Geometrie, Arithmetique, Astronomy (wherein they are verie skillfull as by them held to be the worthiest science of all others) Musique, shootinge, fencing and active feates of the boddie generallie. The best performer holdeth the place of preferment and rewarde for three yeares, and then cometh to a newe triall as before, wherein if hee be excelled by anie one, the better doer carrieth the place, and hee removed. This course is soe dulie observed that parci=
alitie cannot creepe in, and maketh men that have gotten the seate of preferment as carefull to continew themselves therein as they were industrious at y first to mount vp to it.

Printing

1614. September — China

A Cirtuitinig (as they reporte) hath byn vsed amongst them 1800 yeares at the least.

The king maintaines greate state and cometh verie sildome abroad but is continuallie amongest his woimen, being attended vppon by Eunuchs (by them called Ticams). None of his Nobles dare looke him in the face when they speake to him. But the king willing to giue audience being in a roome they speake to him made rounde with glasse windowes the petitioner cometh vnder the windowe, and falleth downe with his face on the grounde, and then speaketh what hee hath to saie, yf hee looke vpp it is as much as his life.

Concerninge the comodities of this Countrie they are Rawe silke, the best are at Lanking, and are called Howsa, and will cost there at Lanking 80 R. of 8 the Picull. Taffatie (called Tue) the best is made at a small towne called Huchu, and will cost there 30 Rs. of 8 the Corge. Damask (called Trone) the best are made at Canton, and worth there 50 Rs. the Corge.

Sewing silke (called Couswa) worth in China 100 Rs. the Picull.
Imbrodered hanginges (called Locy) the best 10 Rs. the peece.
Sewing gould (called Kimswa) is solde by the Chippaw whith is a bundell conteyninge 10 papers, each paper 5 knotts will cost there two roialls of 8 the 3 Chippaws, the best hath 36 threades in a knott.

Sattens (called Lyn) the best one royall of 8 the peece. Greate Basons (called Chopau) will cost 1 R. 3 basons.
White Sugar (called Petongs) the best 1 ¼ R. of 8 the Picull.
Purcelane or stoneware of China in small sortes, (called Poa) the best will cost 1 R. of 8 the 100 peeces.
Pearle Boxes (called Channab) the best 5 R. the peece.
Velvetts (called Tangoiounck) of 9 yardes long 5 R. the peece.
Sleaue silke (called Jounck) the best 150 R. the Picull.
Muske (called Saheo) 7 R. of 8 the Catty.
Cashes, will cost there 60 Peeces for a Roiall of 8.

Comodities vendible there

Broade cloth (called Toloney) the Sasock whith is ¾ of an ∞∞ English yard is worth 7 Royalls of 8.
Looking Glasses verie large (called Kea) worth 10 Rs. the peece.
Tynne (called Sea) worth 15 R. of 8 the Picull.
Wax (called La) 15 Rs. the Picull.
Musketts (called Cauching) the barrell 20 R.
Japan Cattans, or sables (called Samto) 8 Rs. the peece.

Elephants

1614
September

yedzo.

Eliphantes teeth, the greatest best requested, 200 R° y̌ Peecull and small teeth, 100 R° the Picull (called Ga)

White Saunders (called Toa wheo) the best in greate logges is & worth 40 R° the Picull —

The Custome of Pepper inwardes is 1 Taiel vppon a Picull and outwardes noe Custome.

Item the carryinge of munition out of the land is forbidden and strictlie lookt vnto.

In March the Junckes bounde for Manillia departe from Chanchu in fleetes sometimes 4. 5. 10. or more together as they fall readie.

Theire lading outwardes is rawe and wrought silkes which are farr better then they bringe to sell at Bantam.

Item betweene Canton and Manillia it is teen daies sailinge.

In the beginninge of June they returne from Manillia. theire lading homewardes is R° of 8.

Yearlie there goeth to Manillia 40 saile of Junckes at the least, & theire forte is nothinge to be rekoned of, soe that they maie bee taken with a Shypp boate.

Pepper hath of latt yeares byn runn at the souls in China, for 6½ Taieles the Picull when at the same time in Bantam it was to be bought for 2½ R° of 8. the Tribang.

Yedzo

Intelligence concerning yedzo deliuered in the citie of Edoo in Japan, by a Japanner who had bene there twice and reported as followeth v₂t

yedzo is an Island   That yedzo is an Island and lieth on the N. W. side of Japon, and distant from thence 10 leagues.

That the people are white and of good condition, but verie heare-all theire bodies over like Munckies. Theire weapons are Bowes and Arrowes poysoned. The people in the Southermost parte thereof doe vnderstand waight and measure, whereof within the land 30 daies Journey they are ignorant.

They haue much siluer and sand goulde whereof they make payment to the Japanners for rice etc.

Rice and Cotton cloth of Japan is heere well requested.

Iron and leade is brought to them from Japan.

Necessaries for the Bellie and the back are most vendible to them

Rice

1614
September

Japan

Rice transported from Japan to Yedzo hath yeilded fower for one

Matchma. The towne where the Japanners haue theire cheeff residence and mart is called Matchma, there mart 500 howsholdes of Japanners whoe likewise haue a forte there, the Governour whereof is called Matchma donna/

This towne of Matchma is the principall mart towne of all Yedzo, whether the nationalls most resorte to buy and sell especiallie in September for theire provision for winter/

In March they bring downe Salmon and dried fish of sundrie sortes, and other wares, for which the Japoners barter; which the Japonners rather desire then silver/

The Japonners haue noe setled being or trade, in anie other towne then Matchma/

People of lowe Stature further to the N:ward/ That further to the N:warde uppon the same land, are people of verie lowe stature like Dwarfes/

That the Yedzoes are people of the stature of the Japonners, and haue noe apparell but what is brought them from Japan/

A Current to ye East north east. That there setteth a verie violent current betweene Yedzo and Japan which cometh to Corea, and setteth to the E. N. E./

That the windes are for the most parte as usuallie they are in Japan viz: That the Northerlie windes begyn in September and end in March, and then the Southerlie windes begyn to blowe/

Japan

Certen obseruations of matters hapening and passed at Ffirando during the time of our aboade there/

August the 19. Anno 1613 This night began theire greate feaste, the Pagans invitinge theire deade kindred, bancketing and makinge merrie all night with Candle light at theire Graues. This ffeast continewed 3 daies and as many nightes, And verie strickt comand was given from the king that euerie howse should grauell the streete before theire doores and hange out Candle light in the night/ And, as wee were informed, a poore man was put to death, and his howse shutt upp for disobeyinge heerein. The China Captaine furnished vs with two paper Lanthorns verie decent, and fitted for the purpose/

The 23 of August, they made an end of theire greate feast, and 3 Companies of damsells went upp and downe with flagges or banners, theire Musique being drumes and Panns. At the sowndes whereof

1614.
September

Japan.

whereof they daunced at everie greate mans dore, as alsoe at all theire Pagods or Temples and Sepulchers.

The 24 of August 1613 This night all the streetes were hanged with candell light, for that the yonge king and his brother with divers noble men went with a Maske to daunce at the old kings howse. The young king and his brother were on horsback, and had Canopies carried over them, the rest were on foote. Theire Musique was Drumes and kettells as aforesaid and our phifes.

The 28 of September wee intending to burie one of our people, theire Bonzy or priest would not suffer vs to passe through the streete (with the deade corpes) before theire Pagod or Temple, soe that wee were inforced to carrie it by water, and they waies wee had much to doe to procure out of the countrie people to make the grave for a Christian to be buried in, neither would they lett the corpes be carried by water in any of theire boates, wherefore wee carried it in our owne skiff.

This daie the kinge commaunded that Channells should be made on either side of the streetes in Ffirando to convey away the water, the streetes being gravelled and the Channells covered over with flatt stones which was dispatched in one daie everie one doinge it before his owne dore with wounderfull diligence and expedition. Our howse was not the last, Our Landlord setting men presently in hand with it.

October 2 About 11 at night the ould kings howse on the other side of the water was fiered (by casualtie) and quite burnt downe to the grounde in the space of one hower. I never sawe a more vehement fier for the time. It was reported that it was his owne doinge, by going vpp and downe late in the night with lighted Canes, the coales whereof fell amongest the matts which tooke fier.

The 4th of October Reportes were spredd through the towne that the divell had answered by theire Oracle to theire Bozes or coniuringe Preest that the towne of Ffirando should this night be burned to ashes, soe that the criers went vpp and downe the streetes all night makinge such a noise that fewe could take any rest. They gaue warninge that everie one should put out theire fier, but (God be thancked) the divell proved a liar, for no such thinge happened.

The 10th of October kinge foyne came suddenlie vnto vs, as wee were at Dynner and fell to eating with vs. Hee desired to haue a peece of English beefe, and another of Porke sodd with Onions and turneps

1614
September

Japan

turnipps and sent to him the next daie, which was sent with a bottell of wine and halfe a dozen of white bread, which hee kindely accepted, having invited to the eating therof, the young king his Grandchild and Nabisone his brother, with Semidone his kinsman Nota. The first of September, The ould king with all the nobility, made a maske, and the night following went to visitt the younge king his Grandchilde with musique and Drums and kettles, all the streetes hanged with Lanthornes hee wasattended vppon an accompanied wth 3000 people at the least./

The 7 of September 1612 in the night hapned such a Tuffon or storme that never anie of vs had seene the like, neither could anie of the Naturalls remember that ever they had knowne the like. It over threwe above 100 howses in Firando, and vncovered manie other, among which the kings howse was one, and blewe downe a long wall which inclosed the young kinges howse. The sea went so high that it vndermined a greatt wharffe or key at the Dutch howse, brake downe theire stone wall tarried away thirt staires, sunck them two barkes, and 40 or 50 other barkes. The towne did shake therewith, as if it had byne an earthquake wee never passed a night in such feare for the people vnrulie, did rann vpp and downe the streetes all night with feir brandes, that the winde tarried great coales quite over the toppes of howses, and some howses being cleane tarried away with the storme, it whirled vpp the fiers (that were in them) vpp into the aire in greate streames verie feartfull to behould, where with wee feared that the whole towne would haue bene consumed, which doubtlesse had soe byn, but that there fell soe much rayne, (contrarie to the nature of a Tuffon or storme) with lightening and thunder. Our shipp ridd with fiue ankers ahead, yet was shee with the violence therof driven ashoare and wracked diuers of theire vessells which ridd asterne her laden with comodities ffor which theire losses they never demaunded any satisfaction from vs.

At Langasaque it did more harme then heere, ffor about 20 China Junckes, togither with the Spanish shipp that brought the Embassador from the Philippinas, were cast away there./

October 12. 1613 Heere was another great fast amongst the Pagans being (as wee were tould) like vnto the lent amongst the Papistes Captaine Cox and our English Marchants were invited by Captaine Brower to the Dutch howse, where they had greate cheere well drest both after the Japan and Dutch fashion, being serued vppon tables, but had noe carowsinge, or inmoderate Drinkinge.

1614.   Japan.

September

The ould king sate at one table accompanied with his eldest sonne and both the younge kings brethren (for the younge king hymselfe was not there). At the other table first sate Nabesone the ould kings brother, and then Captaine Cox, and next him Semydone, and next him the ould kings Governour, and divers other Cavalleros on the other side.

Captaine Brower (whoe was as mayster of the feast) did not sitt at all, but carved at the tables, his people and servaunts attending and serving on theire knees. In the end of the Dynner, Captaine Brower gave drinck to everie one of his guestes with his owne handes and uppon his knees which seemed strange to our English: whoe (when all was fynished) asked him what hee ment to kneele to the Japannors (they sitting at table) hee answered that it was the fashion of the Countrie, And in case the king hymself made a feast, Hee did the like for the more honor of his Guestes.

A greate Eclips of the Moone

October the 18, being mundaie. At Firando was a greate Eclips of the moone, it begann about 11 of the clock at night, and was totally obscured.

The 19th. In Firando were 40 howses burnt downe, and many more had followed had not our Englishmen lustelie bestirred them, for which the king and the people much commended them.

They feared a greate fier shortlie to followe, theire Divell and Conjurers (as they said) having tould them thereof.

The 23 of October 1613. The people of Firando held a greate feast, both the kings, with all theire Nobilitie accompanied with divers strangers, mett together at a Summerhouse, which for this purpose was sett upp before the greate Pagod or Temple to see a Horse race. There went about 3000 persons assembled. The noble men ridd thither attended uppon with a rowte of slaves, some with pikes, some with small shott and others with bowes and arrowes. The Pikemen weare placed on the one side of the streete and the shott and Archers on the other side, the middest of the streete being left voide for the runinge of of the race. Right before the Summer howse (where the kinges and nobles sate) was a rounde buckler of strawe, hanged against the wall, at which the Archers on horsback (runing as swiftlie as theire horses could carrie them) dyscharged theire arrowes.

Archers on Horsback

About tenne of the clock this night, the Captaine Chinesa (our Landlord) knockt at our dore, giving us to understand that the king had given expresse command, that every howse should have a tubb of water readie in the upper partes thereof, for that the Divell had said the towne should this night be burned. Wee gott a greate tubb of water of some 20 buckets on the topp of the howse. Menn did run upp and downe the streetes all night long, bidding everie one to looke to theire fier. It was strange and terrible to us to heare them and much disquieted us, but in the morninge, the Divell was found a lier againe.

1614.
September

Japan.

The 24 of October wee went as the former night, deyed with these ovens of fier, before it was kindled, wherefore doubting the worst wee provided buckets, ladders &c whereof wee had noe vse, praised be God.

The 30 of October our landlord toulld vs of a generall Collection which was made through the whole towne howse by howse of Presents of eatable comodities for both the kinges, for the more hono[u]r of a greate feast they were to haue the next daie, with a Commodie or Play, wee prepared two bottells of Spanish wine, two roasted hens, a roasted pigge, a small quantitie of rusk, and three boxes of Bankettyng stuff.

Before night the young king sent one of his men to Captaine Cox, requesting him to furnish them with some English apparell for the better grating of theire Commodie, and pticulerlie a paier of Stammett cloth breeches, whereof wee had not any.

within night both the kinges sent and invited Captaine Cocke and the marchaunts to the seeing of theire stage playe or Commodie on the morrowe.

The 31 of October wee sent o[u]r Present before vs mew and requested pardon for not coming to the playe, but they would take noe excuse, wherefore wee went, and founde a place appointed and reserved for vs where we satt and sawe all at our pleasure The ould king Foyne him selfe came and brought vs Collation in sight of all the people, and when hee had ended Semidone came and did the like in the name of both the kinges. And after that divers noble men came and made vs a third Collation. But the matter held by vs most note wor thie, was theire Commodie the Actors being the kinges them selues w[i]th the greatest noble men and princes The matter acted was of the valient deedes of theire Auncestors from the beginninge of theire kingdome or Common wealth vntill the present wherewith much mirth was intermixed to delight the spectators, the number beinge greate for there was not a howse in the towne, nor any villedge or place in theire Dominion but sent a Present and were spectators The kinges them selues did see, that everie one both greate and small did eate and drinck before they departed Theire Actinges, theire Musique and singinge, seemed vnto vs verie harsh, yet kept they due time both with handes and feete

Theire instruments of musique are little Tabo[u]rs small in the middle and greater at both endes like to an howerglasse, they beatt the one end with out of theire handes and straunt ietten cordes which are spand about it, with the other hand, which doinge they make it to sounde greate or small, highe or base as them listeth Tuninge theire voices thereto, another playinge with a phife or flute, but all harsh
and

1614
September.

Later intelligence from Iapan.

and vnpleasant to our hearinge.

At our returne to the English howse wee founde 3. or 4 flemmyngs there, one of them being in Iapan habit, and was come from a place called Tushma, within sight of Corea, where (as wee vnderstand) they had sould pepper and other comodities.

A Dutchman came from Tushma

November the 3. 1613. The night past, three howses were sett on fier in divers partes of the towne, but soone quenched, soe that little or noe hurt was donne. But for the time to come order was nowe given to take notice of everie howse what people lodged therein whether strangers or els, and such as should be founde to be suspected to be banished out of the Countrie. And Gates or barres were made to shutt vpp the passages, and endes of streetes, and watch sett in divers places, noe man to be suffered to walke in the night vnlesse his occasion be extraordinarie and a light with him, hereby was taken awaye that ryngyng of fier, and makinge of noize vpp and downe the streetes in the night time which heertofore soe much did vex and troble vs.

Notwithstandinge these good orders A villaine about 10 of the clock in the night did sett a howse on fier neere vnto the Pagod, over against our English howse, but being espied by the watch hee fledd into a wood a little distant from that Pagod, which presentlie was besett rounde about with about 500 Armed menn. The ould king Foyne himself being there in person with many noble men who assisted in the pursuite, but hee escaped them all.

Alterations hapned in Japan since my departure thence, and whereof I have receaved intelligence from Captaine Richard Cocks, by his lres, dated in Firando in Japan the 10 of December 1614. as followeth viz.t

That the Emperor hath latelie banished all Jesuitts, Priestes, Friers & Nunns (professing the Christian religion) out of Japan, hath pulled downe and burnt all theire Churches and Monasteries, and hath shypped the Jesuitts &c. out of his dominion, some for Macau in China and others for Manillia.

That the ould king of Firando Foyne sama is dead, and that Vshiandono his Governour, and two of theire servaunts

1614
September

Later intelligence from Iapan.

did rypp open theire owne bellies to hasten theire endes, that they might beare him companie in the other world, whose bodies being buried, theire Ashes were in tombes together with his/

That warres are begun betwixt Ogoshosama the old Emperour and Fidaia sama the younge prince, sonne to the former Emperour Taico sama otherwise called Quabacondono/

That Fidaia sama had fortefied himself stronglie in his castell of Ozaca, having fowerscort or one hundred thowsand souldiers, (Runawaies, banished men and malcontentes) retired out of all partes vnto him and victualled themselves for three yeares, Whereuppon Ogoshosama himself in person came downe against them with an army of three hundred thowsand souldiers. And was in December 1614. at the Castell of Fushma, theire forerunners having had divers skirmishes, and many on both sides slayne/

That by reason heereof, the greate cittie of Ozaka is burned to the grownde all saving the Castell, and parte of Sackay likewise/

That such a Tuffon or Tempest did about that tyme happen at Edo, that the like had not bynn seene within the memorie of man, the sea did overflowe all the cittie and drove the people from thence vpp into the mountaines, defaringe and breaking downe all the howses of noblemen, and other monuments which were most costlie and beutifull/

And as concerninge trade, they had sould a good quantitie of theire broadclothes and other English comodities (since the departure of the Cloaue) for good proffitt, and better should haue donne, but that the Hollanders by the putting of of theirs at base rates, enforced our English factors to conforme themselues somewhat in price to them/

That had not these warres hapned Captaine Cockes had greate hope to haue procured trade into China which hee doubted not to effect for three shippes yearelie to come and goe to a porte neere Languin whether they might saile (with a good winde) from Firando in 3 or 4 daies/

That Jacob Speck a Hollander who was thought to be cast away in sailing from Japan to the Molucas was returned to Firando Captaine of a great shipp, called the Zelandia with a little Pinnasse called the Jaccatra. The most of his soe long missinge was for that the shipp wherein hee went from Firando passed to the Eward of the Philippinas (the same waie that the Cloaue passed to the from the Molucas to Japan) yet by Currants and contrarie windes (as they reported) could not fetch ye Molucas,

1614   Later intelligence from Iapan.

September

but were driven to the westward of the Island Celebes, and soe passed rounde about it through the straightes of Desalon, and soe back againe to the Molucas p[er]e

That the Chinas doe much complaine of the hollanders for robbing and pilfering of theire Iunckes havinge (as they saie) lattlie rifled and taken 7.

That the Emperor of Iapan hath taken some distaste against the hollanders, and did refuse a Present which they lattlie sent upp to him, not once vouchsafinge to speake with those that brought it. The like hee did to the Portingalls who came in the greate shipp Anno. 1614. from Amacau to ∞∞ Langasaque neither acceptinge theire Present, nor gravinge them with accesse into his Presence.

That everie shipp which ariveth in Iapan must send upp a Present to the Emperour as a Custome. Neither may any sett out a Iunck without procuring the expresse and yearlie licence of the Emperour, without which noe Iapan Mariner dare to goe out of the countrie vppon paine of death. But strangers shippes maie come and goe out when them listeth, and noe main reprove them.

That our English could not as then (by any meanes) obtayne trade from Tushma into Corea neither have those of Tushma any other priviledge, but onelie to enter into one little towne or fortresse, without the walles whereof, to the Landward, they dare not under payne of death to goe.

The king of Tushma is noe subiect to the Emperor of Iapan. Our English factors could vent nothing but pepper at Tushma, and not greate quantitie thereof. The waight is much more then that of Iapan, but afforded at a better rate.

That upp in the countrie of Corea they have greate Citties, betwixt which and the sea are mightie and spatious Boggyes, whereuppon none can travell on horsback, and verie hardlie on foote. For remedie against this inconvenience they have

Wagons that Sayle.

greate Wagons or Cartes which are carried and drawne vppon brwade or flatt wheeles, theire motion caused by sailes gathering winde as that of shipps, soe that observing the Monsons and generall windes they transport theire goods to and fro in these sailinge wagons. In these partes of Corea they have Damaskes, Sattens, Taffaties, and other silken stuffes beinge made there aswell as in China.

That

1614
September

Later intelligence from Japan.

That it is reported, that Taicosama (otherwise called ∞ ∞ ∞ Quabicondono) the deceased Emperour did intend to have conveyed a greatt Army of souldiers in those sailing Wagons, to have assaulted the Emperour of China, on a soddaine in his greate cittie of Paquin, where ordinarilie hee is resident. But hee was prevented by a noble man of Corea whoe poisoned himselfe to poison the Emperour, and other greate men of Japan, whereby the Japanes lost all that, which 22 yeares past, they possest in Corea.

Finis

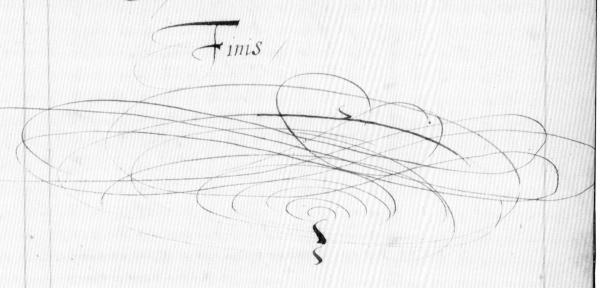

Blood not eat at Fushimi see 1613 Aug.t 29th

27

解　説

平野健一郎

概要

　本書の原本の著者、正式なタイトル、刊行年は、John Saris, *The First Voyage of the English to the Islands of Japan*, 1617 である。原本は手筆本、小さなフォリオ判1冊、31.4×21.4㎝、121頁。金の装飾で縁飾りされたベラム装である[1]。用紙はヨーロッパ産である。原本を東洋文庫が所蔵する。1952年7月19日に、種別「書跡・典籍」、名称「ジョン・セーリス日本航海記〈自筆本／西暦1614年〉」で重要文化財の指定を受けている（指定番号第1537号）。東洋文庫では特別貴重書に分類され、請求番号はPB-30である。

標題、内容と依拠原本

　標題は *The First Voyage of the English to the Islands of Japan*（「イギリス人による日本列島への最初の航海」、もしくはジョン・セーリス『日本渡航記』）である。内容は、イギリス東インド会社の第8回東インド航海の司令官ジョン・セーリス（1579/80-1643）が、クローヴ号、ヘクター号、トマス号3隻の船団で、262人の船員を指揮して行った航海の記録である。航海はイギリスからジャワ島のバンタムへ、さらにクローヴ号のみによってバンタムから目的地、日本の平戸にまで至る往復の航海であった。記録は、1611年4月18日、イギリス・ダウンズ出帆から始まり、1614年9月27日、イギリス・プリマス帰港で終了した航海の、「航海記録」（log）にとどまらない。セーリスが平戸と駿河・江戸の間を往復して、徳川家康・秀忠に拝謁し、与えられたジェームズ一世への返書と貿易特許状など、航海期間中に得た資料や見聞を随所に配するなど、「航海記」に近いものに仕立てられている。

　本書が依拠した底本は、東洋文庫が1924年にロンドンの稀覯書店 Maggs Bros. 社から購入することを決め、翌25年に所蔵を確定した手写本の原本そのものである[2]。次に述べるように、いわゆる「ジョン・セーリスの航海日誌」には数種類の異本が存在するが、東洋文庫が所蔵する原本は唯一無二の孤本であって、他の異本に勝るとも劣らない貴重な史料であり、「東洋文庫本」と称されるものである[3]。

異本

いわゆる「ジョン・セーリスの航海日誌」には、次のように、4種類の異本が存在する。

　①イギリスインド省所蔵日誌(海事記録 Marine Records, no.xiv)
　②*The Voyage of Captain John Saris to Japan, 1613*, edited by Sir Ernest M. Satow, London, printed for Hakluyt Society, 1900(ハクルート版)
　③Samuel Purchas, *Hakluytus Posthumus or Purchas His Pilgrimes, Containing a History of the World in Sea Voyages and Lande Travells by Englishmen and Others*, 1625, 1905 に所収の「ジョン・セーリスの航海日誌」(パーチャス版)
　④*The First Voyage of the English to the Islands of Japan*, by John Saris, 1617(東洋文庫本)

　①は、イギリス東インド会社の会社記録を引き継いだはずのインド省が所蔵する「日誌」であり、Marine Records, no.xiv という番号が付されていることからしても、「ジョン・セーリスの航海日誌」の原本中の原本であると考えられるかもしれない。現に、アーネスト・サトウがハクルート協会のために編集した②のハクルート版は、この①を底本とする活字本ということになっている。サトウ自身、インド省所蔵日誌を自分の目で見、その筆跡がセーリス自身のものであることを確認したと述べているが、サトウは日誌を一見したあとは、翻字をインド省の女性職員に、底本と翻字の点検確認をインド省のインド史研究者に託したという。インド省所蔵のセーリスの日誌を実見したもう一人の人が、日本で最初にセーリス『日本渡航記』に注目し、研究を促進された日欧交流史研究の大家、岩生成一教授である。岩生教授は1931年にロンドン近郊のフラムにあるセーリスの墓を訪れており、1954年には旧インド省文書部に同部所蔵のセーリス「航海日誌」の1頁目の複写を作成してもらっている[4]。

　しかしながら、①が「ジョン・セーリスの航海日誌」の原本であると断定することは躊躇される。サトウ自身、自分が一見したのは、いくつかの理由から、航海日誌の原本(log)ではなく、写本であったと考えられると述べている。その写本に貼ってある蔵書票からは、写本が19世紀半ばごろにはトマス・ベスト・ジャーヴィスという陸軍中佐に所有されていたことが確かであり、その後、軍事省が購入して、インド省に帰属すべき史料であるとの考えから、1889年にインド省に移管したのであった[5]。岩生教授が後述の村川堅固訳『セーリス日本渡航記』に提供したインド省史料の複写写真を見ても、それは写本の1頁である。そこで、インド省には、その写本と別に「日誌」の原本があるのかどうかが問題となり、また、ジャーヴィス中佐が所持していたことのある写本とはどのようなものなのかも問題となるが、それらは今のところ謎のまま残さざるをえない。そもそも、セーリスが帰朝報告として東インド会社に航海日誌を提出しなかった可能性があることを示す状況証拠も少なくないのである。

②は「ジョン・セーリスの航海日誌」のハクルート版と呼ばれ、今述べた成立事情から「アーネスト・サトウ版」と呼ばれることもある。「ハクルート版」と呼ばれるのは、ハクルート協会(Hakluyt Society)の委嘱を受けたサトウが①を底本として翻刻・編集し、同協会から出版したからである。ハクルート協会は、1846年にイギリスで設立されたブック・クラブで、航海記や外国旅行記を出版することによって海外事情や地理に関する知識を提供し、研究を支援することを目的としたので、名前を航海記、旅行記の収集家兼編集者の先駆者であったリチャード・ハクルート(Richard Hakluyt, 1552-1616)にあやかったのである。このハクルート版は今でも印刷されているようであるが、写本ではなく、別の写本を底本とする活字本であることをあらためて指摘しておきたい。

③は、サミュエル・パーチャス(Samuel Purchas, 1577?-1626)が編纂出版した航海記シリーズで、17世紀までのイギリス人を中心とした世界旅行・航海の記録を収めた全集である。その第3巻の355-519頁にジョン・セーリスの航海記録が収められており、「セーリスの航海日誌」のパーチャス版と呼ばれる。パーチャス自身は旅行も航海もしたことがなかったが、テムズ河河口の港町で知り合った船乗りなどから外国旅行、航海の記録を集め、大量の写本を作っていた。そのようなパーチャスに先行した人物がリチャード・ハクルートであった。ハクルートの収集と編集の助手をパーチャスが務めたこともあるといわれ、ハクルートは1616年の死去に際して、未刊行の資料をパーチャスに遺贈したのである。パーチャスが1625年に刊行した③が、ハクルートによって集められた資料をも含む航海記録集であったことは、その書名からも察することができる。現在手にすることができるパーチャス版は活字本であり、それらの原稿(原史料)がどうなったかを確かめる術は今のところない。

東洋文庫本の特徴

さて、複製底本である④の東洋文庫本は、セーリス自らが制作した手写本(マニュスクリプト)であり、美しい手筆の原本である。これがロンドンの稀覯書市場に出されたときの Maggs Bros. 社のカタログは、この写本の特徴を次のように述べていた。「**一六一一年から一三年、イングランド―日本間、最初の公式航海の手書き日誌。司令長官セーリス艦長が書いて、フランシス・ベーコン卿に贈ったもの**」、「**セーリス艦長自身が書いた航海のオリジナルな手書き記録**」、「**一二一頁からなる一巻で、当座の日誌ではなく、おそらく帰国後、余暇時間に書かれ、そして英国国璽尚書フランシス・ベーコン卿に特に贈るために、きわめて美しく書かれている**」、「**手稿は小さなフォリオ判で、原本のまま、金の装飾で縁飾りのあるベラム装**」である(太字は原文の英文のまま)[6]。すなわち、1611年から(正確には)1614年にかけて行われたイギリス―日本間往復の航海について、セーリス自身が「書いた」手書きの日誌・記録のオリジナル版、あるいは手稿そのものであることを強く打ち出していた。これが東洋文庫本の最大の特徴である。現在確認することができない①を除いて、われわれが手にすることができる②ハクルート版、③パーチャス版、④東洋文庫本の3つのうち、写本であ

るのは東洋文庫本だけである。

　東洋文庫本のもう一つの特徴は、Maggs Bros. 社のカタログにもあるように、これそのものがセーリスからフランシス・ベーコンに贈るために美しく作られた手写本であることである。標題頁の次の扉頁は、まさしく国璽尚書ベーコン卿への献辞である。東洋文庫本を復刻するために詳細な書誌学的検討を加えた大塚高信教授は、この事実を手がかりに、*The First Voyage of the English to Japan by John Saris, transcribed and collated by Takanobu Otsuka,* Toyo Bunko, 1941において、東洋文庫本の制作年を次のように推定している[7]。セーリスは帰国後、東インド会社を辞め、1615年には、ロンドン市長だったトマス・キャンベル卿の孫娘と結婚、財政的に余裕のある生活を送った。したがって、自分の航海日誌を清書して、ベーコン卿に贈るつてやきっかけ、余裕は十分にあったであろう。ベーコン卿が国璽尚書に任命された時期から考えて、清書が完了したのは1617年3月から18年3月の間であったであろう。そこで、表紙頁の最後に「1617年」と記されていることとも合わせて、写本(東洋文庫本)の制作年は1617年と確定される[8]。とすれば、未確定の①を除いて、②の出版年は1900年であり、③の出版年は1625年であるから、われわれが手にすることのできるセーリスの「航海日誌」のなかでは東洋文庫本が最古のものということになる。

　1614年9月27日にプリマスに帰港したセーリスは、直ちに東インド会社に帰国報告を行い、積み荷を投資者たちに引き渡すであろうという関係者の予期に反して、なかなかロンドンに上がろうとしなかった。会社が派遣した会計検査官は投資者たちの儲けが200パーセントになると査定し、実際、セーリスの航海は、東インド会社の最初の12回の航海のなかでは2番目の好成績を挙げたばかりか、アジア貿易の見通しを大きく広げた。しかし、セーリスは、自己資金で別取引を行い、自分の貨物を秘かに荷揚げした疑いで処罰されそうになった。このような会社との係争を抱えたまま、1615年には会社を退職し、結婚し、引退してしまったのである。家康などからジェームズ一世に贈られた贈り物などは国王に奉呈したものの、日本から持ち帰った贈り物のなるべく多くを自分のものにし、オークションにかけたともいわれる。

　そうした行為の一つとして、セーリスが自らの航海の記録そのものをより価値の高いものにしようとしたことは十分に考えられる。すなわち、ハクルートやパーチャスがまさにそのとき創り出していた航海記・外国旅行記・探検記・冒険記の出版ブームに自ら参加したのではないか、と考えられるのである。実際、パーチャス版のセーリスの航海記には、セーリスから提供されたと明記された記録資料が含まれている。それ以上にさらに興味深いことは、これまで見逃されてきたが、セーリスがベーコン卿に捧げた献辞そのもののなかにハクルートの名前が明記されていたという事実である。婉曲話法で飾り立てられた中世英語の文章を読み解くと、そこには、セーリスが保管していた航海記をハクルートが見て、公開する価値があるとしたが、ハクルートが死去(1616年11月23日)したために実現せず、ハクルートの最後の配慮でセーリスに戻されたそれを敢えてベーコン卿に献呈する次第である、と述べられているのである。ベーコン卿に献呈するために作られた写本は、本複製で見られるように、美しい書体を最初から最後まで維持した見事な手写本である。清書家とし

て最高のプロフェッショナルが、セーリスの不断の監督を受けながら、時間をかけて、丹念に書き上げたものに違いない。ハクルートやパーチャスたちが創り出していた出版ブームがそのようなことを可能にする環境を提供したと考えられる。

　以上のような4つの異本の成立過程や特徴を踏まえると、セーリスの航海日誌異本の間の先後関係(系統)を推定することが可能となる。大塚教授は、*The First Voyage of the English to Japan by John Saris, transcribed and collated by Takanobu Otsuka* で、異本間の系統の可能なパターンとして、次の4つを挙げている。

　　［凡例］L：原日誌(Log)、I：インド省所蔵本、P：パーチャス版、H：ハクルート版、T：東洋文庫本、
　　　　　　X：存在を仮定する手写本

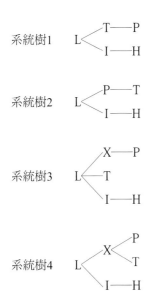

そして、系統樹3か4である可能性が高いことを示唆している。Xは存在を仮定する手写本であるから、同じ原日誌から「インド省のとは別に一つの手写本ができ、その手写本から東洋文庫本と、パーチャスの原稿とが共に別々にできたのであろう」という推定である[9]。ここであえて論理的な仮定をもう一つ加えれば、

　　　　系統樹5　　L―X＜ T / P / I―H

もありえよう。その場合、X＝T、X＝P、X＝Iのいずれかである可能性も含まれる。インド省所蔵のセーリスの「日誌」がL(およびI)であるか否かを確認することが一つのカギとなるが、セーリスとハルクート、パーチャスたちの間にあったと考えられる交友関係と、そして、なによりも東洋文庫本の美しい出来栄えから考えて、X(もう一つの手写本)が(L＝Xではないとしても)かなりの期間、セーリスの手元にあったと想定することも可能であるように思われる。

以上のように、未確定部分を残しながらも「ジョン・セーリスの航海日誌」の4つの異本が出揃ったのは、1614年から1625年の間と考えられる。イギリスにおける航海記ブームに含まれる期間であった。通常、異本の間の先後関係を考証し、系統樹を推定することは、原典を確定する（そして、原典に最高の価値を与える）ための作業であるが、この「ジョン・セーリスの航海日誌」に関してはそれは該当しないと考えられる。なぜなら、航海記ブームのなかで新しい情報が加えられることによって、後からの異本に史料としての価値が加えられることになったからである。東洋文庫本は、原日誌を除く3つの異本のなかでは完成年が最も早く、唯一の写本であるが、セーリス自身が制作に関わったものである。セーリスが航海記ブームのなかに身を置いて、おそらく3年以上かけて作り上げたことが、東洋文庫本を会社報告用の航海日誌から「日本渡航記」に高めることになったのは、後世の人々にとって幸いであった。

東洋文庫本の内容

　本複製本で見られるように、東洋文庫本は、扉頁の次の頁（3頁、本複製本では19頁）からの本文部分では、大枠として原本の航海日誌の形式を維持している。すなわち、各頁の左側に年月日の列を設け、「1611年4月18日」などと記入し、続けて本文部分にその日の「ダウンズ出帆」というような航海事項を記している。船の進路、移動距離、水深、天候、そして特に風向と船から見える沿岸の地勢と島の形状を丹念に記入している。日々の日誌の最後には、船員への「給与」と船員に与えた飲食物を詳細に記録しているのも目立つ点である。

　東洋文庫本の外形的な特徴の一つは、各頁の頭の1行にその頁の内容を示す「見出し」が記されていることである。それは、たとえば「イングランドからマダガスカルへ」、「マダガスカル」、……、「モルッカ諸島」、「モルッカ諸島から日本へ」、……、「日本のフィランド（平戸）」、……、「博多の町」、……、「駿河」、……、「江戸の都」、……、「平戸へ戻る」、……、「日本を出る」、……というように、その頁に記録されている場所ないしは場所の移動を標記したものである。それだけでなく、「皇帝の手紙」、「日本における貿易の特権」、……、「後日日本から得た情報」などの標題がつけられた頁も差し込まれている。当座の日誌につけられたのではなく、後の編集段階でつけられたものであることは明らかであり、読者（まずはベーコン卿）の便宜を考えたものであった。同様に、もう一つの特徴も東洋文庫本を航海記として読む人々の需めに応じるものであったであろう。すなわち、各頁の左側の欄外の随所に細字で「小見出し」が書き込まれているのである。それは、該当の個所の数行に書かれている内容を、「われわれは平戸まで半リーグのところに到達した」など、欄外注の形で要約したもので、航海記の読者を関心事項に導く索引の役割を果たすものであった。

　さらに航海記に近づけるために、後から本文中に書き加えられたに違いないものが二つある。一つは、冒頭に"nota"という見出しがつけられた、数行からなるパラグラフとして随所に挿入されている注記である。そこには、碇泊中あるいは訪問先の場所の説明、そこで会った人物の紹介、その

土地の珍しい風習の解説、特記すべき見聞と体験の記録などが追加されている。もう一つは、航海期間に各地で集められた文書記録である。訪問した土地の支配者と交換した文書が英訳され、フルテキストで、しかも同じ書写者の筆跡で、適宜該当箇所に転記されているのである。その代表的な例が、家康から与えられたジェームズ1世への返書と貿易特許状(朱印状)、平戸・松浦藩の先代藩主、松浦鎮信から与えられた感謝状である[10]。狭義の航海日誌には記載されるはずのない注記と文書類が東洋文庫本に含まれているのは、それがセーリス自身によって航海記に変容させられたからであるが、まさにそのお蔭で東洋文庫本は類まれな史書となったといえよう。

　後述するように、セーリスの「航海日誌」には村川堅固訳『セーリス日本渡航記』という、日本への渡航部分についてはほぼ完璧な日本語訳が存在する。その訳書は、上記4つの異本のうち、②を翻訳の底本とし、③と④を十分に参照しながら作られているが、読者の便宜のために、原典②、③、④のいずれにもない章分け(航海の時期区分にも相当する)を施している。セーリスの「航海日誌」の全体を把握するために、また、特に本複製本全体を見通すために便利なので、同訳書の目次を摘記すると、以下のとおりである。

　　第1章　イギリス出帆よりバンタムまで(1611年4月18日から1613年1月12日まで)
　　第2章　バンタム出帆よりタワリ島まで(1613年1月14日から3月11日まで)
　　第3章　タワリ島よりモルッカ諸島まで(1613年3月12日から4月13日まで)
　　第4章　モルッカ諸島より平戸まで(1613年4月14日から6月10日まで)
　　第5章　平戸(1613年6月11日から8月7日まで)
　　第6章　平戸より江戸へ(1613年8月7日から9月12日まで)
　　第7章　江戸より平戸へ(1613年9月14日から11月6日まで)
　　第8章　司令官が皇帝の宮廷に赴き、不在中起れることについての商務員頭マスター・
　　　　　　リチャード・コックスの記事(1613年8月7日から11月6日まで)
　　第9章　平戸(1613年11月7日から12月5日まで)
　　第10章　平戸を出帆してイギリスへ向かう(1613年12月6日から1614年9月27日まで)[11]

　この目次を、東洋文庫本の特徴の一つである各頁頭部の「見出し」と対応させてみよう。訳書第1章は、大きく縮約されているが、東洋文庫本では、最初の"From England to Madagascar"(本書19頁)から"Bantam"(55頁)までに相当する。つまり、イングランドからバンタムまで、アフリカ大陸沿岸部沿いから中東、インド洋を通過して、東インドに到達するまでの、冒頭4分の1の重要な航海の記録は、東洋文庫本でこそ詳しく読むことができるのである。

　以下、平戸到着後、日本滞在中の期間に限って見れば、訳書第5章に相当するのは、"Firando in Iapan"(84頁)から"The towne of Fuccate"(93頁)の頁の途中まで、第6章に相当するのは、"The towne of Fuccate"(93頁)の途中から"The Pilgrimage to Tencheday"(100頁)までである。この部分に駿河で家

解説　153

康に拝謁したときの様子を記した記事がある。第7章に相当するのは、"The Cittie Edoo"(101頁)から "Our returne to Firando"(107頁)までである。ここに、"The Emperours letter"と"Priuiledges for trade in Iapan"の見出しの下、家康の返書と家康から与えられた朱印状の英訳文が収められている(102頁と103-104頁)。訳書第8章はセーリスのものではない別の文献から訳書に取りいれられた史料なので、それに相当する部分は東洋文庫本にはない。訳書第9章に相当するのは"Our returne to Firando"(107頁)の頁の途中から"Our Factorie left in Iapan"(108頁)までであり、第10章は"Our returne from Iapan"(109頁)以降である。松浦鎮信からの感謝状は、帰路のバンタムで英訳されて、"Bantam"の部分に"The King of Iapan's letter"(114頁)の見出しで掲げられている。歴史研究の新しい光が当たるのを待っている史料が少なくないように思われる。

東洋文庫への収書の経緯

本複製本の原本が東洋文庫に収納され、「東洋文庫本」となった経緯については、従来、1917年から1924年までの間に岩﨑久彌氏が稀覯本の一つとして購入したものとされていた。1917-24年は東洋文庫の「モリソン文庫仮事務所」時期であり、モリソン文庫を購入したあと、増補拡充のために稀本を購入していた時期であった。ところが、この点については、すでに大塚教授が、東洋文庫本全体に関する考証のなかで、1924年にロンドンのMaggs Bros. 社の *Bibliotheca Asiatica* 上に写本が広告されると、東洋文庫はすぐさま書店に電報で注文を発し、購入に成功したのであると断定していた[12]。その根拠は、Maggs Bros. 社の広告と、東洋文庫本の複製・翻刻を委嘱された際に、大塚教授が東洋文庫の責任者(岩井大慧氏と思われる)から直接その話を聞いたという事実である。東洋文庫はセーリスの航海日誌を1924年に購入し、翌25年に所蔵を開始したと確定してよいであろう。広告に「イングランド—日本間、最初の公式航海の手書き日誌」とあったことが購入決定の決め手になったのに違いなく、それは千載一遇、見事に的を射た決定であったといえよう。

復刻、翻訳の経緯

東洋文庫本は、1940年に東洋文庫によって、ジョン・セーリス著『影印セーリス航海日記』(1940年、121頁)として複製された。したがって、今回の複製本はジョン・セーリス『航海日誌』の2度目の復刻に当たる。戦前の東洋文庫は、開設から終戦にいたる20余年の間、独自に覆刻本シリーズを企図して、所蔵する孤本稀書を選んで覆刻し、専門研究者による解説を付して限定出版するか、「東洋文庫叢刊」シリーズに収めて出版した。本書の復刻本は「東洋文庫叢刊」の(10)として刊行された[13]。東洋文庫が復刻を委嘱したのは東京文理科大学英語学助教授(当時)の大塚高信教授(1897-1979年)であった。

大塚教授は続けて、*The First Voyage of the English to Japan by John Saris, transcribed and collated by*

Takanobu Otsuka（1941年、289頁）を「東洋文庫欧文論叢3」として刊行した。当時、大塚教授はシェイクスピア時代の英語の専門研究者として実績を挙げていたが、この書で、東洋文庫所蔵本と、先に記した異本のハクルート版（アーネスト・サトウ版）とパーチャス版の3書の間できわめて入念な校合（コレーション）を行い、その成果にもとづいて、東洋文庫本の最初から最後までを完璧に翻刻（トランスクリプション）したのである。大塚教授による上記「東洋文庫叢刊」（10）の復刻本とこの「東洋文庫欧文論叢3」の校合・翻刻とを併せて、東洋文庫は「モリソン文庫仮事務所」時期以降の「増補拡充事業で購求ないし複製した稀本の影印と解説文ないし邦訳」[14]の一点を追加しえたのである。今日、われわれは、2度目の複製本である本書と1941年の大塚教授による翻刻とを併せ見ることによって、セーリスの『日本渡航記』の英語原文を正確に読むことができるわけである。

　しかし、大塚教授の功績はそれにとどまらない。大塚教授の無私の働きがなければ、セーリス『日本渡航記』の日本語訳はなかったかもしれないのである。今日、われわれには村川堅固訳『セーリス日本渡航記』（雄松堂、新異国叢書6、1970年）という日本語の名訳の定本が与えられている。西洋史学の泰斗村川堅固教授は、昭和初期の一夏を費やしてセーリスの「航海日誌」の仮訳を一応終えたが、多忙と中世英語の難しさで未完成のままの原稿を10余年間放置せざるをえなかった。1940年、東洋文庫本の復刻作業を終えようとしていた大塚教授の訪問を受けた村川教授が旧訳稿を示したところ、大塚教授は訳稿を完成させることを申し出、あまつさえ、原稿が完成したら適当な出版社を見つけ、公刊することも約束したのである。1944年9月、村川堅固訳『セーリス著日本渡航記』（十一組出版部、1944年）が出版された。村川教授は、自分の訳書が公刊されたのは「まったく大塚氏の一方ならぬ義俠的援助のたまものにほかならず」と、「甚深の謝意」を表した[15]。戦後1970年に刊行された新異国叢書中の村川訳『セーリス日本渡航記』の主要部分は、この1944年出版の訳書をほぼそのまま踏襲したものである。村川教授はもともとハクルート版を底本として訳出を試みたのであるが、刊行された村川訳では、ハクルート版とパーチャス版、東洋文庫本との間で異なるところがあるすべての個所に注が付され、異なる文章の訳文が示されている。この丹念な作業に大塚教授の翻刻と校合の成果が完全に活かされ、東洋文庫本の復刻と翻刻および村川訳書の完璧な三位一体が日本に生まれたのである。セーリス「航海日誌」に対する日本人関係者の貢献が、英語でも得られない成果を残していることは特筆に値する。われわれは、本複製本によって原典を追いながら、大塚教授の翻刻によって現代ローマ字でそれを確認し、村川教授の訳書の本文と注のT（東洋文庫本）印の訳文を続けて読んでいくことによって、セーリス「航海日誌」の東洋文庫本ヴァージョンを存分に味わうことができるのである[16]。

本書出版の意義

　本書は、世界史的な意義を有する「ジョン・セーリスの航海日誌」の、世界唯一の写本である東洋文庫本の復刻本である。底本である東洋文庫本について、『東洋文庫八十年史I——沿革と名品—』

（東洋文庫、2007年）は、二つの意味で貴重な史書であることを挙げている。一つは、日本とイギリスの国交開始に関する重要な史料である点、もう一つは、ジョン・セーリス等の日本滞留日記であり、彼らの目に映じた当時の日本の姿を伝える、貴重な日本近世史の海外史料である点である[17]。17世紀初めの日本社会を外国人が見た記録として、ほかに例の少ない史書である。特に、平戸の人々と混ざった生活の様子、駿府・江戸への旅行中に垣間見た庶民の様子は、ほかでは得られない記録として、この上なく貴重である。加えて、フランシス・ベーコンに献呈した手書写本[18]の実物を伝えて、今後も世界の書物学史上に意義を発揮するであろう。

　最後に、今回のこの複製本は、東洋文庫所蔵のジョン・セーリス『日本渡航記』の2度目の復刻であるが、最新の複写技術を駆使して「ジョン・セーリスの航海日誌」の東洋文庫本を鮮明に復刻し、世界の人々の参照をより容易にするであろう。最初の複製・翻刻が戦時中(1940-41年)の日本で行われたことは奇跡といってもよい歴史的な事績であるが、イギリスをはじめとする世界に十分伝わったとはいえないようである。今回の複製によって、東洋文庫本はあらためて世界的な重要文化財として知られ、参照されるようになるであろう。そうすれば、この解説で未解明のまま残された問題も国際的に究明されることになり、戦前から日本で先人たちによって積み重ねられてきた文献整理と研究の業績の上に、ジョン・セーリスの「航海日誌」に対する新たな研究が進むに違いない。

典拠

The First Voyage of the English to Japan by John Saris, 1617（「東洋文庫叢刊」(10)ジョン・セーリス著『影印セーリス航海日記』），Toyo Bunko, 1940, 121ps.

The First Voyage of the English to Japan by John Saris, transcribed and collated by Takanobu Otsuka, the Toyo Bunko Publications Series D, Volume III（「東洋文庫欧文論叢3」），1941, 266ps.

The Voyage of Captain John Saris to Japan, 1613, edited by Sir Ernest M. Satow, London, printed for Hakluyt Society, 1900.

Samuel Purchas, *Hakluytus Posthumus or Purchas His Pilgrimes, Containing a History of the World in Sea Voyages and Lande Travells by Englishmen and Others*, originally 1625, Glasgow, J. MacLehose and Sons, 20 vols., 1905-1907.

Cyril Wild, ed., *Purchas His Pilgrimes in Japan* extracted from *Hakluytus Posthumus or Purchas His Pilgrimes* and edited with commentary and notes, Kobe, 1938.

村川堅固訳『セーリス著日本渡航記』十一組出版部、1944年9月。

村川堅固訳『セーリス日本渡航記』雄松堂、新異国叢書6、1970年。

金井圓訳「アーネスト・サトウのハクルート版への巻頭言と序説」、村川訳『セーリス日本渡航記』雄松堂、1970年、附録三、281-380頁。

A Classified Catalogue of Books on the Section XVII. JAPAN in the Toyo Bunko acquired during the years 1917-1956, Toyo Bunko

史料・参考文献

岩井大慧編『東洋文庫十五年史』東洋文庫、1939年

榎一雄『東洋文庫の六十年』東洋文庫、1977年

『東洋文庫八十年史I——沿革と名品——』東洋文庫、2007年3月

『東洋文庫の名品』東洋文庫、2007年3月

平野健一郎「奇跡の書——東洋文庫蔵ジョン・セーリス『日本渡航記』の書物学的考察——」東洋文庫『アジア学

の宝庫、東洋文庫——東洋学の史料と研究——』勉誠出版、2015年3月、107-127頁

ティモシー・ブルック、藤井美佐子訳『セルデンの中国地図——消えた古地図400年の謎を解く——』太田出版、2015年

高野彰『洋書の話』第二版、朗文堂、2014年11月

注
1) この2行にまとめた原本の基本特性は、後述するMaggs Bros. 社のカタログの要点である(ただし、東洋文庫の採寸による版の実寸を除く)。判型については、後掲の村川堅固訳『セーリス日本渡航記』(雄松堂、1970年)の「解説」395頁は「小型四折本」としているが、ここでは、英文カタログおよびToyo Bunko, *A Classified Catalogue of Books on the Section XVII. JAPAN in the Toyo Bunko acquired during the years 1917-1956*, p.100 にしたがって、「フォリオ版」(2折本)とした。
2) 後述の大塚高信教授の考証による。
3) 念のため付記すれば、「東洋文庫本」とは、東洋文庫にのみ所蔵されている原本の意であって、平凡社の同名シリーズに収められている一書ということではない。
4) 村川堅固訳『セーリス日本渡航記』(雄松堂、新異国叢書6、1970年)、岩生成一「校訂者のことば」3-4頁。
5) 以上のような、①のハクルート版の成立事情、すなわちインド省所蔵のセーリスの「航海日誌」とハクルート版の編者であるアーネスト・サトウの関わりについては、サトウのハクルート版への巻頭言と序説に述べられている。「ハクルート版への巻頭言と序説」の金井圓訳は、村川堅固訳『セーリス日本渡航記』新異国叢書版に「附録三」として収められている(特に、281-285頁を参照)。
6) この英文カタログのほぼ全文が大塚高信教授によって、*The First Voyage of the English to Japan by John Saris, transcribed and collated by Takanobu Otsuka* の序文第1頁に書き写されている。
7) *The First Voyage of the English to Japan by John Saris, transcribed and collated by Takanobu Otsuka*, the Toyo Bunko Publications Series D, Volume III(「東洋文庫欧文論叢3」),1941, 289ps., p.xviii. 大塚教授の絶大なる貢献については、次々項以下で詳しく触れたい。
8) 重要文化財指定書は成立年を1614年とし、『東洋文庫八十年史Ⅰ——沿革と名品——』東洋文庫、2007年と『東洋文庫の名品』東洋文庫、2007年もセーリス『日本渡航記』の東洋文庫本の制作年を1614年とした(56-57頁)が、これらは1617年に訂正される。
9) *The First Voyage, transcribed by Otsuka*, preface, p.xviii. なお、大塚教授自身の系統図は東洋文庫本の符号をBとしたが、Tに改めた。
10) 松浦鎮信からセーリスに宛てた感謝状の原文は、漢文で書かれていた。セーリスはこれを帰路のバンタムで、中国語とマレー語ができる現地人に翻訳させ、漢文→中国語→マレー語→英語の経路で重訳させたのである。なお、ジェームズ1世が家康に宛てたといわれる書簡は、国王の署名入りではあったが、宛名はもと空欄の、友好と交易を求める趣旨の定型的な書簡で、セーリスは東インド会社からそれを4通与えられていたという。バンタム到着以前の前半の航海中に、アフリカでそれを使用した形跡もあり、家康には同様の1通に宛名を記入して差し出したものと考えられる。したがって、「ジェームズ1世の家康宛国書」という表現は、厳密にいえば正確ではない。
11) 誤解を避けるため、年号の一部分を修正した。
12) *The First Voyage, transcribed by Otsuka*, preface, p.i. 今回、この解説の執筆にあたって、東洋文庫に現存する図書購入台帳の大正10年から大正15年までの2冊(「図書原簿」自大正十年至大正十三年および「European Books」大正十二年〜昭和九年)をチェックした。大判皮装、特製の台帳に丹念なペンマンシップで記入された購入・収書記録を精査したが、著者名「Saris」、書名「The First Voyage ……」の項目を見つけることはできなかった。考えられる原因は、別の台帳が存在したか、特別購入であったためにこの台帳に記入されなかったか、であろう。他方、*A Classified Catalogue of Books on the Section XVII. JAPAN in the Toyo Bunko acquired during the years 1917-1956*, p.100 には書誌情報が正当に記載されているが、購入・収書の情報は含まれていない。現在のところ、「東洋文庫本」の誕生時期に関する大塚説を却けるに足る証拠は見当たらない。

　話を複雑にする怖れがあるが、当時の東洋文庫が「セーリスの日本渡航記」を購入する明確な意図を

持っていたことを示すエピソードをここに記しておきたい。東洋文庫のホームページの「蔵書・資料検索」バナーのなかにある「図書資料の検索」の「I　書誌」の「類別検索」の欄を開き、「(3)欧米語資料」のなかの「大正時代の購入書籍リスト（洋書）」を探ると、その692番に

"De reys van Kapitein Johan Saris, etc. van October 1605, tot October 1609"
"Saris, J."
1部／大正7年7月26日／丸善
セーリスノ日本紀行ノ和文ナラン要調査

というデータが記載されている。資料のタイトルに記入された1605年10月から1609年10月という年月からして、これがセーリスの平戸への航海に関したものでないことは明らかである。実は、平戸への航海はセーリスにとって2度目の東インドへの航海の一部であって、セーリスは1604年から1610年まで、東インド会社の第2回東洋航海に参加して、彼自身1回目の東インド航海を行っていたのである。このオランダ語資料はその時のセーリスの航海についてであった。東洋文庫はこれも購入しており（貴重書O-9-10、O-9-11）、「要調査」の注意書きに東洋文庫がセーリスの「日本紀行」に狙いを定めていたことが読み取れる。

13) 『東洋文庫八十年史I』および『東洋文庫の名品』、いずれも20頁。
14) 同上。
15) セーリス著、村川堅固訳『日本渡航記』十一組出版部、1944年9月、訳者序2頁。
16) セーリス『日本渡航記』の翻刻・校合と翻訳の経緯について、より詳しくは、平野健一郎「奇跡の書──東洋文庫蔵ジョン・セーリス『日本渡航記』の書物学的考察──」（東洋文庫『アジア学の宝庫、東洋文庫──東洋学の史料と研究──』勉誠出版、2015年3月）107-127頁、特に116-119、124-126頁を参照されたい。
17) 『東洋文庫八十年史I──沿革と名品──』（東洋文庫、2007年）56-57頁。同様に、『東洋文庫の名品』57頁も参照。
18) 重要文化財指定書は「自筆本」とし、『東洋文庫八十年史I』と『東洋文庫の名品』は「自筆稿本」としている。しかし、東洋文庫本の冒頭にあるベーコン卿への献辞に付されたセーリスの署名は、セーリス自筆とされているサインとは明らかに異なる、整った書体である。この点からも、古書店の広告文にかかわらず、「自筆」は厳密に受け取られるべきではなく、代書人による（すなわち、広く「人の手で筆写された」）写本と解するのが適当である。

謝辞
　戦時下における故大塚高信教授の真摯なお仕事が残されていなければ、私にはこの解説の執筆に手をつけることすら不可能であった。時代を越える学恩に心から感謝を捧げる次第である。実際の執筆に際しては、東洋文庫図書部、研究部の瀧下彩子、橘伸子、山村義照、徐小潔の皆様にさまざまに助けていただいた。江南和幸龍谷大学名誉教授にセーリスの写本の用紙を確定していただき、大井剛東京成徳大学教授に書誌事項についてご指導を賜った。郷健治神奈川大学教授にはシェークスピア時代のイギリスの出版・書写事情について教えていただき、原写本の筆跡を鑑定していただいた上、カギとなるセンテンスを訳読していただいた。記して感謝の気持ちを表したい。

東洋文庫善本叢書 第二期 欧文貴重書 3

重要文化財 ジョン・セーリス『日本渡航記』
Saris, John: *The first voyage of the English to the Islands of Japan, 1617.*

2016年12月28日 初版発行

監　修　東洋文庫
解　説　平野健一郎

制　作　(社)勉誠
発行者　池嶋洋次
発　売　勉誠出版(株)
　　　　〒101-0051　東京都千代田区神田神保町 3-10-2
　　　　TEL：(03)5215-9021(代)　FAX：(03)5215-9025
　　　　http://bensei.jp

印　刷　㈱太平印刷社
製　本　若林製本工場

© Toyo Bunko 2016, Printed in Japan

ISBN978-4-585-28223-5　C3080

東洋文庫善本叢書 第二期 欧文貴重書

全3巻セット(分売可)・本体 205,000円(+税)

ラフカディオ ハーン、B. H. チェンバレン往復書簡
Letters addressed to and from Lafcadio Hearn and B. H. Chamberlain.

平川祐弘 [解題]　　　　　　　　　　　　　　2016年10月刊行・本体 140,000円(+税)

日本研究家で作家のラフカディオ・ハーン(Lafcadio Hearn, 小泉八雲 1850-1904)は、帝国大学文科大学の教授で日本語学者チェンバレン(B. H. Chamberlain 1850-1935)の斡旋で松江中学(1890)に勤め、第五高等学校(1891)の英語教師となり、のち帝国大学文科大学の英文学講師(1896-1903)に任じた。本書には1890-96年にわたってハーンがチェンバレン(ほか西田千太郎、メーソン W. B. Masonとの交信数通)と交わした自筆の手紙128通を本邦初の全点影印。多岐にわたる内容を有した往復書簡の肉筆は2人の交際をなまなましく再現しており、西洋の日本理解出発点の現場そのものといって過言ではない。

『東方見聞録(世界の記述)』1485[?]年刊ラテン語版
Polo, Marco: *The Description of the World* Latin edition translated by Francesco Pipino, 1485[?]

斯波義信 [解説]　　　　　　　　　　　　　　2016年11月刊行・本体 25,000円(+税)

この書は1298年、マルコが作家のルスティッケロに東方大旅行の見聞をヴェネチア方言で口述し、後者がそれをフランコ・イタリアン方言でまとめて成った。たちまち広く流布するが、転写や訳出で使われる言語の問題によって、6種類の異本テキストが立ち並びつつ伝世した。その中で、1310年代、ボローニャのドミニコ会士のピピノ師がラテン語で訳出したピピノ本とその系統は、国際教養語であるラテン語のテキストなので信頼され、活版印刷の時代に入って早くも1485年[?]に出版され、頼るべき底本として最もひろく伝わった。かのコロンブスが世界周航に先だって、今回の覆刻本の僚本を所持し、欄外に多くの書き入れを残し、いまもセヴィラのコロンブス図書館に蔵されている。本書はG. E. モリソンの旧蔵をへて東洋文庫に伝わり、朱墨印刷の美麗な稀本である。東洋文庫にはモリソン文庫以来、80余種類にのぼる《東方見聞録(世界の記述)》の異種刊本、異種訳出刊本を備えている。

重要文化財 ジョン・セーリス『日本渡航記』
Saris, John: *The first voyage of the English to the Islands of Japan, 1617.*

平野健一郎 [解説]　　　　　　　　　　　　　2016年12月刊行・本体 40,000円(+税)

ジョン・セーリスは国王ジェームス1世の命をうけ、帆船クローブ号で船員80名弱を率いて平戸にやって来た。駿府、江戸において家康や秀忠に面会して、王の親書を奉呈し家康の返書、ならびに通商免許状と土産物をうけて帰国した。本書は1611年4月18日英国ケント州ダウンズ港を出帆してより、1614年9月27日プリマスに帰帆するまでの航海および日本滞留日記で、しかも時の英国大法官フランシス・ベーコン卿に献呈した手写本である。日英国交開始に関する重要史料であり、また、上記の道中においてセーリスの目に映じた当時の日本の姿を克明に伝える、日本近世史の海外史料として重要な役割を演ずるものである。